To R.G.H who always knew I would.

NOT A SURVIVAL GUIDE

Synergy Publishing
Newberry, FL 32669
publishwithsynergy.com

Not A Survival Guide
By Nicole Howes

Printed in the United Kingdom.
International Standard Book Number:
ISBN 9780912106427

Design by Ian Howes

FSC

NOT A SURVIVAL GUIDE

Your straight talking
parenting companion.
Navigating the shift
from child to teen.

Nicole Howes

Synergy
PUBLISHING

Introduction

Chances are, you've picked up this book due to one of the following reasons:

Guilt.
Desperation.
Fear.
Trying to avoid feeling any of the above.

So let us first of all address the most important thing. You have picked up this book because you want to learn. You want to be a good parent or carer to a young person in your life. Maybe you want to do better, or maybe you just want to be armed with as much information as possible as your child approaches their teenage years.

That alone means you are already doing great.

Before we start, I think it is important to provide some context as to where this book comes from and how it can work for you.

This book cannot and will not cover every possible scenario. It cannot account for every teens individual personality, behaviour or their reactions. Whilst a 'fix-all' solution is appealing, I think we all know that would be impossible. Even if I could, I don't believe that teenagers (or your parenting for that matter) need fixing.

I do not profess to be a parenting expert because simply put, I am not. I am an 'on the ground, right in the mix of it', parent to teens. I have days where I feel like I have everything together from a parenting perspective and others where I am barely holding on.

Instead of a guide, consider this book a companion, to provide you with some tools to help you through this stage of parenting, to offer insight and a sense of community. To spark conversations. You are not alone. This book is created in such a way that you can pick it up and read it from cover to cover, or as life tends to get in the way some of the time (who am I kidding, all of the time), should you decide to read sections as and when they become relevant to you, that works too. It's your journey.

Some elements throughout will work as gentle aids but needn't be followed to the letter. Most are created to encourage you to look at things from a different perspective or more appropriately, a wider angle.

Importantly, this book is not a survival guide, indeed the clue is in the title. I do not believe that teenage years are there to be 'survived'.

They are to be lived and loved, just like all the other stages of parenting that you have already passed through and have come to, I would bet, look back on with fondness, even if they were incredibly challenging at the time. I am not insinuating it will be an easy ride, but maybe that's part of the fun of it.

Nicole x

NB: For the teen that has just picked this up and thought WTF. This book has been designed with straight talking in mind, so if you are a curious teen there is absolutely no need to put it down. There are no secret tactics to coerce you into 'good' behaviour. Your parent, relation or caregiver is not trying to get one up on you by reading this. Trust me, they are simply trying to be the best they can be for you, to help you both to navigate what can be a tricky time. So, read on if you like or pop it back where you found it.

Before we get stuck into it

Right, before we get into it, there is just time for a few house rules. I will refer throughout this book to a "child" as "your teen" for ease of reading. Two things to note here.

Firstly, I have used the phrase teen or teenager for consistency's sake. Take it as a global word for any child from the age of 10 onwards, as when the shift happens, it is more gradual than the films would have us believe. It depends on many factors, including their own level of maturity and their upbringing, it's a very personal experience. I hope that you will find this book useful at many stages of teenhood, from 'pre' through to 'well and truly in the thick of things'.

Secondly, know that this book is an appropriate tool for all those who are a part of bringing up a teenager. Parents, step-parents, grandparents and guardians. Older siblings, those close friends that you call your family, carers, educators and everyone beyond and in between. I will use the term parent(s) throughout, but my intention is that encompasses you all.

You will find short 'letters to your teen' peppered throughout this book, these can be lifted directly from the pages to act as conversation starters, read out loud to them (ideally with a nonchalant approach that doesn't say, "I bookmarked this page last week") or locked into your mind for when they feel appropriate to wheel out. Use your own take on them. Like everything on these pages, they are not set in stone, nor will they work for every family, situation or culture. Take from them what you need and leave behind all that you don't. I won't be offended, so don't overthink it.

I have at times, had huge moments of doubt surrounding writing this book, as if it becomes a marker for my own parenting 'success', allowing myself to get caught up in the myth of there being a set of rules to parenting, which, if we all follow them diligently will enable us to form perfectly rounded, wonderful human beings as they emerge into their adulthood. That this tome will become a measure of my own parental capabilities, a stick to beat me with.

I have woken in the night, plagued by the thought of this book going to press, only for the media to discover that the wheels are at that moment in time, coming off in my own home and my teens are going 'off the rails'. That I am a fraud.

I have expressed this to my husband, on more than one occasion, and he has simply said, "is that not the entire point?". Annoyingly, I suspect he may be right. So, here I am, writing this section as a reminder to myself as much as you.

Parenting is not a skill that we can study and expect to achieve perfection. It is not something that can be taken out of a box and set up. Nor is it the case that those who study it the most, or talk the loudest about it, are the best in their field. It is a journey, as unique as our children themselves. It is not linear and it is rarely easy. It goes without saying that all involved will make mistakes along the way.

Maybe we could all try being less hard on ourselves and others as parents. Let's not forget, this is our first time living our life too.

Your parenting style, it's personal

I have no intention of putting you in a box when it comes to your parenting style and I don't think you should either.

According to many parenting blogs, books and resources, it seems to have been collectively decided that there are four main types of parenting.

These are: authoritarian, authoritative, permissive and uninvolved. Each style pretty much reflects its given name, but in the case of any doubt, here is a little overview...

Authoritarian parents tend to prioritise obedience over compassion resulting in a strict and punishment heavy, "my way or the highway" style regime.

Authoritative parenting sets strong boundaries and enforces rule with consistency, whilst creating positive relationships and favouring praise over punishment. Authoritative parents will talk to their children to help them to understand the consequences of their actions and to help them make better choices in the future.

Permissive parents simply allow their children to do pretty much whatever they want. They have very few boundaries and don't tend to punish or implement consequences for bad behaviour. Permissive parents may suggest rules, but they will rarely follow through with enforcing them.

Uninvolved parenting, as the name suggests, is neglectful parenting. Uninvolved parents offer their children little or no guidance. They do not nurture their children or provide parental attention. Children are left to their own devices most of the time.

Just to confuse matters further, there is also an ever-growing selection of unofficial sub-categories for parenting being thrown into the mix. These labels tend to go in and out of fashion, heightened by social media trends.

Free-range parenting, helicopter parenting, bulldozer parenting, lighthouse parenting, gentle parenting, attachment parenting, tiger parenting, the list goes on.

The thing is parenting is a very personal thing. Your approach (and level of patience) will change, depending on your personal situation. It can be impacted by your financial pressures, your stress levels, how present you are able to be, your mental and physical health and generally how your day has been.

Ask my children and they will tell you, I am a very different person when I am hungry, "Quick, throw mum a biscuit! She's a monster when she's hangry".

Jokes aside, the point is, I don't think parenting is something that can be boxed and labelled. Parenting is a spectrum. We are only human.

If I had to categorise this book, it would probably fall into the authoritative parenting section. Hands up though, I have been both permissive (particularly on holidays, "ice cream for breakfast, yeah, why not.") and authoritarian (cue 7th "why?"... "because I blooming well said so").

This book is not a programme you can follow, a label to add to your parenting techniques, or a badge of honour.

To be clear, that doesn't mean that you will get off completely scot free. Most of this book will actually be about you, well us. There will be home truths, moments of reflection and maybe some bloody hard work.

It is about parenting with consideration. It is about trying to make good choices day by day. Putting one foot in front of the other.

It is about being the parent you are proud to be.

Fuck you, 18 summers

I see the same posts roll around every year on social media, a cutesy reminder that we only have 18 summers with our children. No pressure then guys.

Actually, in recent years this window of opportunity has been shortened further, with the message '75% of the time we spend with our children will be spent by the time they are 12 years old' being broadcast to the social feeds of many a loving parent. Eurgh. As if we don't all have enough on our plates already.

For me, at the point of having children either already in or entering their teens, the whole 'time is not on our side' mantra, started a spiral of thoughts.

75% of our time with our children has already passed.
We will no longer have the time to bond further.
Well that's it. It's done.
Their childhood is over.
What if I haven't done enough.
What if I haven't been enough?

I have always tried to 'make the most of every moment throughout their younger years, just like people cited I should - I really did. Scared to blink in case I missed it. Mainly because everyone told me that they grow up 'too quick' and they would be 'horrible teenagers' before I knew it.

Then, suddenly we were right there. Staring the 'horrible teenager' stage in the face. Shit.

What if I haven't got it right? Oh man, and what if I really mess up in their teens?

gasp Will I be the reason they are sitting in a therapist's chair in 10 years time?

When it had been time for my son to say goodbye to primary and head up to high school, I had gladly waved him through the gates (from a safe distance, so as not to embarrass him, you understand) pleased and content in the knowledge that he would have new opportunities and experiences ahead. He was definitely ready for the challenge.

As my second child, my daughter, approached the end of primary school though, it hit differently. It is no exaggeration to say I felt bereft. Like I was in freefall. I knew that it felt out of kilter with reality but I couldn't move from it.

At the end of the day, I knew my daughter was growing up. She had outgrown her little village school long before this point, and was more than ready for this next stage of her journey. Yet, this feeling of loss wouldn't shift. It felt raw, like a deep ache in my chest. Ebbing away.

It wasn't until I was driving along, listening to a conversation on a podcast, that I realised it was possible that I was experiencing some form of grief, triggered in part by the transition from one period of parenting to another, exacerbated by the expectations I had. This was all being amplified by the level of pressure placed on us by society and in turn ourselves.

So why was it affecting me so deeply this time around? There is of course a chance that by this point in time, I now had experience of what those 'horrible teenagers' were really like, the ones that everyone had warned me about. Maybe it's just that I couldn't face it a second time (I jest).

So, how did I recover? It is less dramatic than it sounds, but it actually took for me to have a car crash to snap out of this spiral. Nothing major thankfully, but it was enough to jolt me awake pretty quickly. A stark reminder to pay attention to the moment and stop looking forwards or backwards. It brought me back to parenting more consciously.

As our children approach their teenage years, how many of us look back and feel like we didn't do enough? How many people lose precious years thinking beyond the day we are in, constantly considering the 'what ifs'?

The real question is, 'what is enough being measured against?'

When you look at it with a clear frame of mind, are your children happy and safe? Do you love them? Do you want the best for them?

Then in my book (which happens to be this one) that's enough.

> **At 13** " It will ALL work out beautifully. Just trust and be kind to yourself.

Collective strength

As we journey through this book together, you will notice, it is far from linear. Much like parenting.

We are fooled into thinking that life is set out that way, especially those who grew up as little girls. Our heads are filled with rom-com fantasies and Disney-esque ideals. Find the love of your life, get married, have children and then... erm.

As I have aged, I have discovered that life is not about following a set of rules in a certain order. That tends to leave us pretty miserable, putting us at risk of just following the motions and forgetting to actually live in the moment. Life is not an A to B journey.

As I have mentioned and the title alludes, this book is not written as a guide, it is a companion. So, with that in mind, I couldn't create it without having some honest conversations with other humans.

Throughout the process of building this book, I have made a conscious effort to talk to lots and lots of parents (and teens). It felt important to create a safe space where we can all be heard, in order to create a book that actually connects and has the ability to support you. I have been fortunate to speak to many wonderful people, all from different walks of life, many with one thing in common, raising teenagers. Some have been friends and acquaintances, some have been strangers that have heard about the project and wanted to have a chance to speak.

Almost everyone I asked was happy to talk. Not all were happy to put their name to it though. Some felt they would be judged for being a bad parent, but I promise you, no one said anything that surprised me during these conversations. No one said anything that I felt was unrelatable. It was honest and real. And it made me feel seen. Some conversations really struck a chord, leaving us all a little emotional and we unpacked it together.

I have weaved these stories/snippets and quotes throughout the book, and named them 'Around the table', because that is for the most part where we were. Sitting around the table with a cup of tea. Akin to those moments that you usually have with only your nearest and most trusted. For me, until I started this book these raw conversations were only happening with very close friends, normally after a cocktail (or two), or as evening moans and analysis with my husband.

But sitting, listening to others, in a sober and open environment, has been remarkable.

I have learnt so much throughout the creation of this project, mostly from talking openly and without judgement towards other people's parenting experiences.

When I embarked on this process, I knew it was something I needed. I knew it would be cathartic and a learning exercise for me as an individual and I hoped it would in some way support the next generation of teens, but I totally overlooked the effect it would have on the other parents I spoke to. I totally underestimated how much people need to be heard.

I met Carla at a book launch, she was there as a self-proclaimed plus one. Thanks to a friend's introduction, we got around to discussing this book. I was reluctant to say too much about my own project, as we were there to celebrate a very different cause, but it turned out that Carla had raised teenagers, so she understood where I was coming from. The moment I explained what I was trying to achieve, she began to open up to me. Carla told me about her son and the struggles they had experienced during his teenage years. She told me how hard it was, how isolated she had felt and how she never really felt like she knew what she was doing. She told me that at times she was terrified, as she felt like she was losing her son.

Carla went on to say that, now in his 20s, the pair are closer than ever. As Carla left the event that evening, she came to say goodbye. She took my hand, looked me directly in the eyes and thanked me, on behalf of all parents for what I was doing. It was a bit emotional actually, which you should know is not like me, but I was really touched.

At that moment I realised I wasn't just writing this book for me. I am writing it for us. All of us.

Many of the parents I have spoken to have voiced the same feelings. Most, upon answering my questions, have thanked me. Many have experienced an emotional response as they recall moments and feelings that they have never been asked about. It almost feels like a project in itself. The aftermath of teen years. The processing of whatever they bring.

> **❝** **I wanted to leave a message, I've been thinking about your questions all day long. They have been kind of going around in my subconscious. So I just wanted to say thank you, because it's been like a process all day long, and I realised I had been carrying all that guilt around. Through answering those questions I had an opportunity to let go of that guilt.** **❞**

During these conversations, I have heard the words 'grief', 'bereft', 'scared' and 'lost', time and time again. Yet when we talk about the teenage years from one parent to another, we often approach it with sarcasm or feigned joy at not having toys to trip over anymore or playdates to organise. It turns out, most of us actually miss those toys. The thing is words like grief and bereft don't seem to fit. We of course have not lost the child we are referring to, they have just changed. Grown.

It does feel like a form of grief, yes, and yet it is mixed with pride, joy, wonder and gratitude. Oh and stress, plenty of stress. Maybe it needs a word of its own. Suggestions encouraged.

I digress, back to these conversations. I have stitched elements of each, throughout the book, in their raw form. I hope they will allow you to see that whilst our journeys are very different, just like our children, that there is comfort in our togetherness. It may offer you some respite to know that there are a huge amount of people going through the same journey, at this very time. Inevitably some days are easier than others. There is also a community of parents that have already passed through this stage, that are rooting for you, who are also more than happy to help and offer advice if you ask.

Reach out, have these conversations with others. Let's normalise and recognise that parenting teens is not easy, but it doesn't have to be unsupported. That, like during all stages of parenting, sometimes it doesn't feel natural. That sometimes you feel sad, angry or resentful. That sometimes you don't want to be at someone's every beck and call. Sometimes, you just want to tell everyone to fuck off and hide away from the world, with a good book, a large mug of tea and a bar of chocolate (that can't just be me).

"You notice it first when there are less toys around. The obligatory trip to the toyshop at Christmas stops. Sometimes I look at her, and I just see it in her face. It's the baby face that has gone. They go from baby face, to little girl and then it changes to teen. The way she carries herself. It makes me feel, I guess 'bereft' is the wrong word, but I don't know how else to describe it. I would love to just go back and sit with that little 3-year-old, just for a little bit. I would love to spend time with the little girl that's amazed by something you have made in the garden, for some imaginary play. I'd love to go back there. I'd love to go back and hold them as babies. I just miss that parent to child bond, and it feels like it's changed overnight. It's no one moment, just a collection of little ones."

AROUND THE TABLE

Whilst our conversations often meandered, there were two main questions I asked everyone. If you want to it's worth writing down your own responses to these questions. Allow yourself some time to reflect on the answers.

"When your child hit their teen years, how did that shift from childhood make you feel?"

_____

_____

_____

_____

_____

_____

"What did your 13-year-old self need to hear?"

_____

_____

_____

_____

_____

_____

Alone in the crowd

I just wanted to forge a little space here.

Parenting can be lonely. Whether you have support around you or not. Especially if your friends do not have children, or their ages don't align.

It can feel like you are giving every part of yourself to others.

If you are feeling lonely whilst bringing up your teen, I see you. We all do.

If you feel alone, don't be afraid or ashamed to ask for help.

> **"I miss everything and I miss nothing. I loved him through every time and every moment of him. I love being his parent"**
>
> **AROUND THE TABLE**

Horrible teenagers

OVERHEARD

"It's those teenagers that are the problem. They just don't have any respect at all nowadays. 20 years ago, you called the police to deal with these kids and they would have had authority over them. Now they are just doing whatever they want, whenever they want. They have dreadful attitudes. No respect for the police, or their parents. They just vandalise everything, drinking, smoking and terrorising everyone and they are only getting worse."

If someone constantly told you that you were off the rails or judged you for being moody, petulant, badly behaved or rude before getting to know you, how would that make you feel?

I have lost count of how many people said to me and my children as they approached their teen years "Oh, you won't know what's hit you once they reach teenage years" or "Ahh, I don't envy you, having a house full of teenagers" or my personal favourite "Teenage years, harder than a newborn with none of the rewards".

Let us just think for a moment of the potential impact of the usage of this language.

I grew up in an era dominated by Kevin, the petulant teenager played by Harry Enfield, who changed quite literally overnight into a 'horrible teenager'. Transformed from a sweet 12-year-old, bouncing around the lounge, in anticipation of his approaching 13th birthday. He was so excited. On the strike of midnight Kevin's happy nature immediately falls away, as his parents acknowledge him "losing his power of rational thought, and the use of his arms", which from this point onwards, lay limp at his side, as he stomps from place to place. Grunting and wailing, Kevin then takes to telling his parents that he hates them and his birthday presents suck.

For my teenage years I carried, like many others, the burden of Kevin's catchphrase, "UHHHH. It's so unfair". I'm not saying it wasn't funny or (at times) incredibly accurate, but it made me feel small whenever adults would joke about that scene to me. It made any feeling I was having, which were sometimes too big for me to handle, feel belittled. If I felt angry or annoyed I was often not given time to talk about it, because it was just a 'teenage reaction'.

It was expected that I would be moody, even before I was, and as a result any feelings that I had were often dismissed as 'oh that's just her being a teenager'.

At 10 years old, my daughter turned to me genuinely fearful after a conversation with another adult and said "I don't want to turn into a horrible teenager. I like who I am".

We have to be aware of the language we are using. We shouldn't be imparting stereotypes upon teenagers before they have had a chance to show us who they are, as an individual. Of course as teenagers they can be moody, they can also be insightful, funny and talented. For that matter, I've also met plenty of moody adults, myself included.

Let's all try to make less sweeping statements directed towards teens and their parents, let's eradicate 'it's just a phase' or 'that's typical teenage behaviour.'

The fact is, often the traits that we see in our teenagers, those that are considered to be less desirable, could actually be the foundations of what will make them incredible adults.

Single-mindedness becomes drive
Egocentric becomes independent
Outspoken becomes honest and candid
Angry becomes passionate
Challenging boundaries becomes tenacious

Think back to your own teen-self. Can you see how your traits have mellowed and/or matured since then? Maybe you actually behave in a similar way as you always have, but those same traits are just more accepted away from the constraints of youth. Do you still carry those labels?

That said, I hear you. As a parent who is barely holding on through a mood swing or who is constantly reminded by your teen that you have absolutely no clue what you are doing, these years are rarely easy. It's tough.

Whilst I do believe it is the right thing to stop broadcasting to our teens that "it is just a phase", within the pages of this little book it is ok for us to recognise that of course, much of it is. Shhhh. That's just for us.

As a parent to a teen, we have to know that is the case. It helps to maintain our sanity amongst the parental taxi services and never-ending clearing up. We have to know that all things will pass.

And whilst our teens are out there working it all out, we are here together, trying to do exactly the same thing. Yes that's right, holding our own shit together.

The thing is, it is ok to not actually have any clue what you are doing (damn it, turns out your teen was right afterall), but it does bring comfort to remember that teenage years are just a phase (even if you don't say it out loud).

Just as all of the other stages of bringing up a child have come and gone, so too will these years.

You've got this. WE'VE GOT THIS.

Dear teen,

Congratulations. It's your 13th birthday, and you have just been handed the keys to a supercar.

You've the chance to customise it however you like, and drive it as fast as you want. This car doesn't require you to hold a licence. Great. Just one little issue though, you don't know how to drive yet.

You can have a pretty good go, you can sit in it and adjust the seat. Turn it on and rev the engine if you like, but the catch is, you are going to have to learn how to drive it for yourself. Do you even know where to start?

You can ask your mates, of course, but their advice may not be the most reliable, as they can't drive yet either. Plus, in a weird turn of events, they are all receiving their own supercars too, so most of their focus is on learning for themselves. Some will likely tell you to just floor it, but that would be a sure fire way to crash, wouldn't it?

You could research online, but some of the information is pretty patchy. There is a lot of noise and fake information so it's hard to work out what is helpful and what is not.

You could ask your parents, of course, they have learnt to drive their own supercars in the past, but although similar to yours, their cars are older with slightly different controls. You are not sure they will be able to fully understand what you need. After all, you rarely see them driving their own car to its full potential, maybe it is even locked away in the garage for most of the week.

So, what's the best thing to do? Get in? Try and work it out for yourself?

Maybe the best route is in finding a balance between sources, before you make a decision.

On reflection, and even though you wouldn't like to admit it, you suspect your parent's car was pretty special back in the day, and although there are some differences in the dash controls, the fundamental elements to driving the car are exactly the same. And you asking for their help may even lead to them getting their own car out of the garage a little more often. Which could be fun. Or cringe. You're not sure yet.

And your friends, well they are learning as they go in their own cars, which again are different to yours, but if you talk together you are bound to learn what has been working and what hasn't.

Throughout all of this, be mindful of the power you have at your hands.

Supercars can be incredibly fun, they are powerful. Trust that yours will get you to exactly the place you are meant to be, eventually, but they need to be driven with respect and understanding in order to reach their full potential. You only ever get one of these, so look after it.

Pause for you

So many of us are just running through the motions, planning for the next thing, trying to keep our heads above the water and not really paying attention to the present moment.

This book aims to support you, not to be perfect, but simply keep you on track and present in your teen's life. It is a fact that guilt does not serve you, unless it is prompting you to make a change. For now, try to leave any thoughts that you are a bad parent, that you don't know what you are doing or that you have not done enough, behind you.

Know that we always have time to change our direction no matter how far we have travelled.

Life, if we are to enjoy it to its full potential, is about living authentically as yourself, about following the path meant for you. It is in noticing the joy in the little moments by remaining present.

That's all well and good, if you are young, free and single, right? It becomes decidedly harder to do if you are a parent. Even more so if you are a single parent. Near impossible if you have a child who has complex needs, who requires additional time or support. Combine that with the other elements of your life, fit in your work, an ageing parent and keeping your own relationship fresh and there isn't exactly an abundance of free time to look after yourself. Well unless you count sitting in front of the TV with a pack of Frazzles and a glass of wine 'self-care'? Which for the record, I do.

I visit a wonderful therapist called Kirsty on a regular basis. I am thankful that this is not because I am working through anything huge, instead simply because I believe that your mind needs attention and time to be nurtured, just as your body needs exercise and nutrition. I know for a fact that having someone else to talk to, who is unconnected with my family, makes me a better parent. A better person overall actually. I recognise that this is a huge privilege as sadly therapy is not as accessible as I believe it should be, for all.

I have talked about writing this book with Kirsty for some time now. She works with adults primarily, but also with families and children individually. We were speaking recently of the many cases in which a child's mental health has been dramatically improved, not by receiving therapy themselves but rather as a result of their caregivers receiving therapy or getting the support they need. Does that surprise you?

Kirsty strongly believes that in order to be a good parent you need to prioritise looking after yourself. Self-care is more than just having a bubble bath, although those are also much needed. True self-care is the equivalent of putting your oxygen mask on first during an emergency on an aeroplane. It may feel counterintuitive, but if you do not look after yourself fully, you will not be capable of looking after anyone else.

I suspect, if you have made it this far and are about to embark on or are already experiencing bringing up teenagers, you have either already worked this out for yourself or you are running on empty.

The years ahead will see you navigating some of the biggest adjustments through your parenting journey since that newborn joined you, over 10 years ago. So, let's get fit for what is ahead to enable you to bounce back from the hard days. Taking care of yourself is vital to give you the strength to adapt to new ways of thinking and keep your mind as clear as possible.

If you feel like you need more support than these tips provide you, make sure you reach out to your family, friends or your local support networks, to help you to find a therapist or alternative support.

For those that would just appreciate a moment to themselves, here are a few helpful things you can do, in order to carve out some space and time for yourself amidst the madness. Parenting is hard, no matter the age of your children.

1 Morning pages

This is one of the most useful tools in parenting and life that I have used. It is a simple, free and non-time-consuming practice taken from the methods of Julia Cameron in 'The Artist's Way'. I recommend her full course, but for those struggling with time this element standalone is a time effective way to help you lighten the load in your mind. Julia suggests that every morning when you wake (I keep a notepad by my bed) you simply write three pages (A4) of whatever pops into your mind. It could be a reflection of your dreams, what you have coming up today, thoughts from the week gone, your goals, frustrations, rants or pockets of joy. Don't consider spelling, handwriting or structure. You just need to write. 3 pages only though. No more and no less.

No one sees your morning pages, you don't need to read them back, burn them if you like.

As a parent it can be hard to find a private domain, a space that is only yours. Morning pages offer just that, they should leave you feeling calmer and with a little extra space in your mind to invite creativity, or at least be able to get your teenager out to school that morning, without entirely losing the plot.

Like anything, some practices work for some and not for all. See how it goes.

2 Schedule in time for yourself

With balancing school runs, emotional challenges, risk assessments, chauffeur duties, your own work, cooking, housework and homework, the chances are that you have very little time just for you.

Of course, if you have the time available then an hour or so in front of your favourite film, an exercise class or a mooch around an art gallery, would all be a perfect way to get some 'you' time. However, the reality is that most parents don't have that luxury.

Topped off with the fact that your teen is likely to be staying up later and later, you may end up finding little more than a slither of time for yourself. I am here to tell you to take the slither. Grab it with both hands. It's your slither damn it.

3 Take a mindful moment

Walk to your next meeting headphone free. Really pay attention to what is going on around you. Listen to see how many sounds you can hear. Bird, traffic, chatter. Zone in to each sound individually and then focus on finding the next.

Slip away for a quiet cup of coffee, make it mindful by really considering how it tastes. Pay attention to how the warm cup feels in your hands, how it smells, how the liquid feels as it touches your lips. You get the idea. This levels up with a stealthy bar of chocolate in my opinion, but whatever floats your boat.

Grab five minutes to just breathe; useful when you are in a heated or stressful situation, the '4-2-6 breathing technique' works to settle your mind and reduce feelings of anxiety. It really is very simple.

First, you inhale through your nose for 4 seconds.

Once at the top, you hold your breath for 2 seconds.

Then, slowly exhale for 6 seconds and repeat.

Lovely.

4 Surround yourself with good people

You have probably realised it by now, but when it comes to caring for teens the support options are limited. Long gone are the parent and toddler support group equivalents, even if they did exist for your stage of parenting, you would be hard pushed to get your teen to join you, wouldn't you.

It isn't always easy, but try and surround yourself with those you can be honest with, who will listen to what you are going through and who give you space to just be yourself. Having a strong support system will provide a valuable soundboard and can help you feel less alone.

5 Let go of perfection

Let's say it louder for those at the back. Taking care of yourself is never selfish, it is necessary to prioritise your well-being over the idea of perfection. Yes, that may mean the house is not immaculate. Yes, it may mean that you haven't been able to run your child to 43 clubs this week but burnout is real, and serious. If you are not at your best your teen won't be able to be at theirs.

6 Cut your tech usage

There are more and more studies showing the damaging effects of the overuse of phones, in particular social media. I can confidently say, if you cut the doomscrolling, you will free up more space for good vibes.

7 Prioritise positivity

It's not always easy is it? To see the bright side. Especially when conversations with your teen feel repetitive and tedious. I will talk about the impact of negative bias further along, but the simple take on it is this; try to stay focused on the positives around you rather than dwelling on the negatives.

Practice showing gratitude for the people and things around you even when things are going wrong.

Tell your teens that you are grateful for them.
Tell yourself that you are proud of what you are achieving.
Treat yourself with kindness and you will feel lighter.

8   Connect with something bigger than yourself

Whilst of course it often is, the use of prayer does not need to be solely from a religious standpoint. It can also reflect a connection with spirituality, nature, the unknown or someone meaningful you have lost.

It doesn't matter what your beliefs are, talking to something or someone beyond the life you are living, outside of your bubble, can often help you see the bigger picture in order to focus on what is needed.

Granted, if you have not used prayer or spoken your thoughts, feelings or wishes out loud before, you may feel a little awkward to start with, but taking 5 minutes to speak about how you are feeling or your intentions will often provide clarity. You could make a little wish while you are there too, if you fancy it. You little tinker.

Fountains and drains

> ❝ **Be a fountain, not a drain** ❞
> **- Rex Hudler**

Friendships can be one of the hardest things to navigate through teen years. It takes time to learn who is right for you and who is not, most people are still figuring that out well into adulthood.

Peer pressure can be a challenge, as it has always been, but maybe it is exaggerated now as much communication between teens is carried out via text, meaning the things that have been sent in the moment can be held over teens for years. From photos to conversations, everything can be screenshot and saved, or worse sent on, in just a second or two.

That's right, whilst you are growing up, making mistakes and quite possibly saying the wrong things from time to time, this is all documented.

I can certainly recall many scenarios from my own teen years, that I am glad have had the opportunity to just fade away in the mind, rather than being preserved for the future. It is much easier that way, to pretend that it never happened in the first place. We certainly all make a lot of mistakes when we are maturing. We also often make the wrong choices with regards to the friendships we value.

So what do you do, if your teen is hanging out with friends that are making them feel bad?

I hate to break it to you, but you are no longer in charge of playdates. Therefore, as parents, for the most part you can't do a lot these days, to influence your teenager's friendship groups. Long gone are the days you could ensure your child's bestie had parents you would be happy to share the afternoon with (guilty).

You simply can't have that level of control any more, and nor should you. The time has come for your teen to start to recognise unhealthy relationships for themselves.

To be honest, by the time I hit my 20s, I still didn't have it all sewn up when it came to toxic friendships, or much else for that matter.

During that time a slightly older (and wiser) friend told me of a theory, called fountains and drains, that they had used to 'audit' their own relationships.

She told me "Everyone around you is either a 'fountain' or a 'drain'. It is simple to categorise them, by the energy they give you. If someone is kind, open, honest and ultimately makes you feel good, both when you are with them and also when you think of them, then they are a fountain.

If, on the other hand, someone is negative, uses peer pressure, makes you feel guilty, excluded or generally bad when you are with them, or when you think back to your time spent with them, then they are considered a drain."

This is a great tool to gift to your teens, I wish I had understood the concept earlier, it would have saved a lot of heartache.

If you intend on following the 'fountain and drains' process to audit your own friendships, it is important to remember that other peoples' fountains may not be your fountains and other peoples' drains may

not be your drains. Follow your own instinct and experiences.
I was fascinated by the concept. I remember asking my friend, "So what about people that I would consider a fountain, those that I know are good people, but are going through something that means they are often negative at the moment, or are depending on me too much, are they a drain?"

She answered roughly along these lines, "Well that depends on the overall picture, how they respond to your help and whether you are helping because you want to or because you feel like they are forcing you to do so. If they are genuinely going through something and you are able and willing to support them, then of course you should do so, providing that regardless of this 'moment' they are still a fountain to you.

To be clear, being a fountain is not about being happy all the time or never needing support, we all need that. It is about the choices you make and how your behaviour impacts on others and makes them feel.

Weigh up if they would help you in the same way, should you ever need it, or are they just taking from you all the time. Are they taking advantage of your good nature? If so, then they may be a drain disguising themselves as a fountain. The idea is to surround yourself with fountains and reduce the drains as much as possible."

"Ok, so is that it? Just cut out the drains?" I was eager to get started, but it is never that easy, is it.

"No, that is just a small part of it. The main part is self-reflection. If your friends were to assess their own friendship groups, how would you fair? Would you be a fountain, or would you be a drain? Is there a risk that you are currently a drain to anyone that you consider a fountain? If so, you need to put some work in there."

Indeed, as it turned out, I had to put in some work.

Dear teen,

What if it all came back to you. Would you be treated to pain or kindness?

Imagine for a moment that your life was a reality TV programme, that you were being observed continually. After all, you are the star of the show.

You are monitored everywhere you go and everything you do is recorded.

You become a phenomenon and every Sunday, without fail, people across the nation sit down to watch the past week of your life and dissect it from the comfort of their sofas.

Consider, how would that make you feel? Would you be proud of the footage? Would you be happy to broadcast your behaviour or ashamed? Would there be more highs than lows overall?

Think for a minute, have you made good choices for the most part this week?

No one can be perfect, nor can you control the behaviours of others. However what you do have full control over, is your own response to a situation.

Overheard in the changing room

The language choices that you make around your teen impacts on them and the way they feel about themselves, more than many realise.

I was recently in a changing room and paused to listen as a parent was talking to their teen, as they prepared for prom. Trust me, I had heard ALL the details of the upcoming event whilst trying to disrobe myself from a particularly tricky dress. You know the style, those that even before you put it on, you have no idea how to discern which is the 'head hole' and which is for arms.

Anyway, this slightly reluctant teen was trying on outfits for the big evening, guided by their mother, passing suit, after suit, after suit to try on.

From my state of tanglement I heard my neighbour going through the motions, pulling on an outfit and opening the curtain to show their mother who waited eagerly on the other side.
Cute, I thought. It's a big moment isn't it, preparing to leave school.

But, what I heard following each reveal, left my heart heavy.

"Nope"
"I don't like that"
"That's too grown up and inappropriate"
"It's ok I guess, but that black does nothing for you. It's too harsh"
"No, that looks terrible"
"Ok, that one will do"

The teen barely spoke. Only once actually, to show some level of approval for the final (and seemingly approved) option.

Now I appreciate that this mum could have been shopping all day for this suit. This could have been a reflection of a weary, fed up family that after a day of hunting for the perfect outfit, just wanted to get the job done and go home already. There could have been a number of other factors that I was not aware of. I had only seen a snapshot.

However, the conversation as it happened, is a great example to help us all take stock of the way we talk, not just to our teens, but to one another. Maybe try instead...

"What do you think of that one?"
"I like the fit of that, shall we grab it in another colour to compare?"
"I think I preferred the previous option, what do you think?"
"Wow, I am so proud to see you in these right now"
"You look amazing"
"How does that one make you feel?"

Importantly this goes beyond the direct language you use towards them, but also what you surround them with. You have a choice in the way you speak to and around your teen, and whilst most of the time it probably feels as though they are not listening, it is all going in.

THOUGHT

Do you show kindness in the way you speak to, and about yourself?

Your teen is likely going to grow up listening to people telling them how much they are like you.
Be the good parts. Be kind to yourself. Be confident in your skin.
If you cannot do it for yourself alone, do it for them.

Make time to 'date' your child

Strip it back. Work out your priorities. Build your week back up around what actually matters.

"I don't have the time to spend quality time with my teen."
Then find it.

If you don't feel like you have enough time to spend with your teen, then you need to work out why. Is it due to long hours at work? Is it because you need to keep lots of other plates spinning within the house? Is it because they are now choosing to be out with friends instead?

Whether you are parenting on your own or alongside someone, it's highly unlikely that all you have to think about day to day is your teen.

Parenting is part of life, but it is not every part. You are likely trying to balance your career, dealing with your own health issues, navigating financial worries, caring for someone else, undertaking further education, or just generally trying to keep your head above the water. It's bloody knackering. I am just going to say it once again, in case you had drifted off last time, there is no such thing as a 'perfect parent', so stop trying to be everything, and focus on what matters.

Indeed it does seem like modern day families are struggling more to find time for one another, but forging time with just you and your teen is important above all else. It is a moment of connection that you will both benefit from.

As your teen grows, so potentially does their attachment to their peers. In turn, their connection with you can weaken. That hurts doesn't it?

As a parent you have a responsibility to keep that connection, no matter how hard it is to hold on to. Sometimes it may feel like you are hanging on by a thread, but keep holding on.

Step one is to realign your priorities. If you've gotten this far, then I am betting that you want to maintain the connection with your teen, even though they are undoubtedly going to make it tricky sometimes. Review your week and see where time is being wasted. For example, at the time of writing the average adult spends 4 hours and 37 minutes on their phone everyday. Are you able to cut scrolling in favour of your teen? Maybe you could look to finish 30 minutes early one day a week in order to carve out some quality time, or maybe you could persuade your teen to join you during a club drop off for a sibling and head out for a drink whilst waiting for pick up. It's your week, and for some this will be easier than others, but try your best to free up space for time with your teen.

For me, before evaluating my week I found I was just flying from place to place, squeezing in work on the road, being a taxi service to my teens and no one part of my life was really getting the best of me. I had spread myself too thin. I sat down and reorganised the week, it had become a patchwork of tasks, after school clubs that no one seemed fussed about, and work. So, just like clearing out a wardrobe, I cleared out my week bit by bit and it is pretty straightforward to do.

First establish your priorities and non-movables within the week and remove everything that is not necessary. Then build your week back up brick by brick, prioritising elements that actually matter. Forge time with your teen, time for yourself and time with others that are important to you. Sack off clubs that your teens have outgrown, work commitments you can do without and anything that is depleting your energy that is not worth your time.

If you end up with your week still looking pretty rammed, don't panic. Time with your teens doesn't need to come in droves, but it does need to be dedicated to them and not interrupted by phone usage or other distractions.

An easy way to start is with a conscious effort to ensure that the 'inbetweens' count. For example, talking in the car when you collect them from a friend's house. Instead of texting them that their dinner is ready, go to their room to let them know and then walk back to the kitchen with them. Eat together without technology being present, walk the dog together or pair up for chores. I acknowledge that the last one may be a reach.

Ultimately though, it doesn't matter what you do or what you talk about. In fact, they may prefer to just be silent in your company and that's ok. This is about reminding them that you are here and you being present in the moment.

If you are fortunate enough to be able to dedicate a larger chunk of time to doing something you both enjoy together, that's great. Organise a date.

Since my extreme schedule clear out, I try to 'date' each of my teens at least once a month. That means dedicating an evening to do what they want with just me, whilst my husband does the same with the other. We alternate it meaning each of us gets one on one time with each teen.

We have been to the cinema, set up an at home spa, binge watched a tv show, been for a meal together, done drawing, baked and been to an open mic night. It doesn't have to be fancy, expensive or elaborate. They just need dedicated time with you.

"I absolutely, absolutely hated that moment when the boys hit the teen years and they left childhood, because for me a lot of my identity was wrapped up in their childhood. I knew who I was when I was mothering them, I knew who I was, but when they became teenagers I felt lost because I was like, "Well what am I now? What's the point of me?".
It was around the time that my career took off, which was a blessing, but there was a really bumpy moment where I was going from being a mother and I knew what that was to becoming a comedian.
I'm still both. I always will be both, but it was a way of me letting go of them whilst also redefining who I was. To arrive in myself, in a way. So I found that really, really hard and I did struggle. It was like grief. It was like grief, a deep grief that I had lost them and I'd lost my purpose. I found the same thing happened again when the eldest one left home. I felt like somebody had died and a part of me had died, but then in this dry space, little flowers began to grow again and I saw that those flowers were me."

Olga Thompson - Comedian (and mother)

AROUND THE TABLE

Always listen. Even if you don't always want to hear it

My daughter is currently going through a stage of playing "would you rather". The moment she senses a snippet of quiet in the room, she will fill the space with a question.

"Would you rather have hands for feet, or feet for hands"
"Would you rather it always felt 6 degrees hotter or 6 degrees colder"
"Would you rather always have savoury or sweet foods"

You get the picture. My job is simply to pick.

It would be easy to dismiss these questions. Instead I give them my full thought every time, I ask for additional context "If I choose feet for hands is it expected I would then walk on all fours?", "Am I the only person that notices the change in temperature?", "Can I still steal a mouthful of your food?".

And we talk. Mostly nonsense, I will admit, for a length of time. But at least we are talking. We are carving time out for her to talk, and for me to listen. When the time comes that the questions change to heavier subjects, I hope that she will know whatever they are, I will be there to listen. Because she has tested me, in her own way, and she knows that I care about what she is asking me, no matter the subject.

In case you are curious, it's hands for feet, 6 degrees hotter and savoury foods.

Dear teen,

It is ok to feel unsure
>to not have all the answers
>to feel confused
>to not be ok
>to not be like everyone else.

Dear parent.
Please see above.

Talking with them, not at them

> **"If I try to talk to my teen, all I get is one word answers or a shrug."**
>
> **AROUND THE TABLE**

If the responses you are getting, when trying to strike up a conversation, are little more than a grunt it could be time to check your conversation techniques. That's right, you could be the problem here.

Take stock of what you are actually asking, is it interesting for them? Do you even care about the answer?

It is easy to fall into the trap of asking your teens the same questions, but imagine if everyday your friend asked you "Did you have a good day?" you'd likely respond, "Yeah it was ok."
"What did you do?" Erm. "Same thing I do everyday Pinky."

In reality, when speaking to a friend, you would be more likely to pick up the conversation from a point of mutual interest, or something that you know they have mentioned before.
"How's work going? Are you still feeling a bit underappreciated?"

You are able to ask your friend a more connective question because you understand their situation more deeply, so that's the first step to better conversations with your teen.

Ask advice from them, "Oh I heard about this trend where kids are going crazy for these blue lollies, have you heard of it?"

Ask them about their interests, their friends and the current trends. Ok, so they may still grunt and look at you like you have two heads, but don't give up. It is vital to show interest in their interests, even if they are certainly not yours. "I saw today that the new series of 'triple monkey and the hot sauce' is coming out next month, are you still into that? " (Zero judgement if you actually love this show, of course).

Brick wall

So, you have been trying to engage in interesting conversations with your teen. You've made time to date them this week, but they are having some behaviour issues and they just won't listen to you when you try to help. It feels like you're constantly repeating yourself. I said, it feels like you're constantly repeating yourself.

Skipping school, smoking, drinking, drugs, underage sex - all top the list of worries for parents of teens, as they have done for decades, and whilst of course we should be discussing the dangers and consequences of such extracurricular activities, it seems from conversations I have had with other parents, that the subtle behavioural issues are the hardest and most frustrating to manage. The ones that are arising on a daily basis. Relentless.

You know exactly what I am talking about don't you; telling little lies, being late, leaving stuff laying all over the house, not completing tasks such as homework, negativity and general dishonesty. It's irksome to say the least.

Now believe me when I say, I know that it's frustrating watching your teen make the same mistakes that you did.

I see you, as you try to explain that to them, over and over. Sometimes it looks like it might be going in. Sometimes you think you've finally got through, and of course that may be the case, should the stars align. But the truth is, however much you try, your teens generally don't want to take your advice.

There is nothing more disappointing than watching them start to follow a path that you would not choose for them, or partaking in something that you consider a bad choice. You have been there and done that, so it is natural that you would want to impart your wisdom. But here's the brutal truth, for the most part they don't give a shit about what you have to say. The sooner you recognise that, the sooner you can help get your message through. But how, if they won't listen. By other means of course. I'll be right back.

Dear teen,

If you are still reading this, I am aware that I stated there were no tricks in this book in order to coerce you, this section is the exception, but with good reason.

Your parents are trying to do the best for you, they want to keep you safe and provide you with an opportunity for success. You find it hard to listen to them when they offer up advice. That's not entirely your fault. It's theirs, for being so damn boring, right?

Actually, no. It has been suggested that your brain tricks you into believing that your parents are stupid as you travel through your teens. Maybe owing to 'way back when', when it would have been helpful to stop wanting to hang out with them, in order to give you the push to leave your tribe. You would have been expected to traverse across jungles or deserts and find a new settlement.

Despite what your brain is telling you, I can assure you they are not stupid. In fact if they are reading this book, they are trying their best to retain a connection with you that is going to last. They want the best for you.

I realise you may not see this yet. But you will in time.

It takes a village

Is it me, or does parenting seem like it is getting harder?

Ye old adage states "It takes a village to raise a child". Meaning that in order to successfully bring up a child, an entire community of people is required. To help support you as a parent, to impart wisdom, to provide your child someone to play with and learn from. To educate, inspire and occasionally serve up a hearty meal. Sign me up. So where is this village you speak of, ye smooth-tongued rhetorician. What do you mean they are busy?

Realistically the time of the village has passed. For many, even the support of family elders has dried up, with many grandparents still working into their 60s, or families living further apart from one another.

But that doesn't mean we should give up on the notion of the village.

Whilst our children may pull away in favour of their peers, it is important to retain adult attachments.

Gordon Neufeld and Gabor Mate's book *Hold Onto Your Kids: Why Parents Need to Matter More than Peers* researched the impact of peer attachment.

Albeit a slightly older study, it is probably, in many ways, more relevant now than ever. They suggest that as parents we should be curating an enriching environment that prioritises parents and adult connection, over peers. They believe that parents have a duty to uphold the connection between themselves and their children, and acknowledge that it takes work to maintain.

Of course, friendships are an important part of teenage years, but if teens are only surrounded and taking on the opinions of people of their own age, and these become their only source of influence and information, it becomes detrimental to their health, development and on a wider scale society overall.

Add into the mix social media and before you know it your teen is living in an echo chamber. By that I mean they are surrounded by people who largely think and act in the same way that they do. Social media influence amplifies this, as it is all too easy to silence opinions that do not match your own, simply by the push of a button to indicate you are not interested. Block.

Without guidance from those with experience and maturity, it is hard to grow.

If your teen's main figure of attachment is their peers, this will rival your authority. Gordon Neufeld and Gabor Mate believe that without a secure attachment base we cannot parent effectively because we lose our influence.

So, how do we hold on to this attachment?

Well these were my main takeaways from the book, but be sure to pick up a copy for yourself, to gain a greater understanding;

This is about putting in the work to reclaim or maintain a connection on an emotional level. It is not about what you plan to do, but actually doing it.

- Show warmth and energy in being in the company of your teen.

- Rather than texting or shouting for them when their dinner is ready, go and collect them, walk back to the kitchen with them.

- If you can't be around so much, leave them a note telling them that you will miss them or wishing them a good day.

- Catch their eye when you can, acknowledge that you see them. Give them a knowing look. Smile. Recognise their presence.

- Put away your phone when they are talking to you and engage.

- Spend time together without distractions, such as phones, work, siblings and peers. Find something you both enjoy doing and actually do it together. As aforementioned, take the time to date them.

- If they push you away, tell you that you are 'cringe' or are just generally resistant to your advances, ignore it. You have a responsibility to keep showing up. Be persistent, it will pay off eventually, but it's not going to be an overnight win.

- Parent consciously, in a way that makes you feel proud of yourself. If you were looking back over the last week of parenting, would you be mostly happy with your job? It won't be perfect, but just keep making good choices.

So, if we are not looking to overly promote peer connection for our children, who else could they be spending time with? Well one suggestion is to encourage healthy relationships with other trusted adults.

Consider who makes up your 'logical' family, this could be your parents and siblings, but it could also be close friends, distant family members, the parents of your children's friends. Who are the people that are there when you need them? Who are your fountains?

Now cherry pick those that you know have an existing connection with your child and the willingness and time to help you out, and make an active pact with these people, for them to become a trusted adult in their life. You can play the same part for their teens too, if relevant. Our close friends have a great connection with our children, and all enjoy one another's company. My children consider them way cooler than us, so they are a great ally when we need it. Their children are younger than ours, but I have already promised to repay the favour someday.

The idea is, that should you need an important message getting through to your teen, that they can broach the subject with them. They don't need a script, just some insight into what you are struggling to communicate. The chances are, as an adult and a friend of yours, your opinions will be aligned in any case, but because it is not just you, as a nagging parent trying to hammer a message home, your teen is likely going to be more receptive to this adult.

Equally sometimes, said adults will provide a perspective that helps us, as parents, to relax about certain things, helping us to pick our battles effectively. Sometimes it turns out, we just need a soundboard rather than a reaction.

Of course though, as we have established, teens are smart and they may recognise the coup from the off. But still. Hearing the same message reinforced from another adult may just help them to digest it more easily. Don't overuse this privilege though, or else you risk diluting its effectiveness. Oh and keep your 'I told you so's' to yourself. No one appreciates the smug.

If you prefer a less direct approach, try and create organic situations that allow your teen to spend time with other trusted adults, maybe this simply takes the form of a BBQ at yours alongside adult family or friends. It totally depends on your personal set up and social circles, but it is healthy for teens to spend time with a variety of generations, in order for them to form rounded experiences and to learn to have conversations with people other than their like-minded peers.

Ultimately, if you are not already surrounded by a village, as most of us aren't, create one. Trust me, it won't just be beneficial to your teen, we all need support and community.

> **At 13**
>
> " I wish I had reached out to my parents more. I'd lost my way a little, but I kept things to myself. I wish I had known I could ask for help.

The art of storytelling

Sometimes, as a parent, you can just see it coming from a mile off, can't you. Did you find something in your teens room? A vape maybe? Or perhaps you have seen less than desirable conversations in their messages? Whatever it is, you know something, but they don't know, you know.

So, you know that they don't know, that you know, that they don't know. Enough of that.

Stop procrastinating, you have options.

Firstly, and something that isn't an option, don't overreact. You've likely been in a similar situation when you were young. Teens experiment, they push boundaries and they succumb to peer and social pressure. They have to make their own mistakes. You can't micromanage everything in their lives. They are simply not babies any more.

That said, if you have found something that means your teen is in immediate danger, then of course you should talk to them and put measures in place to ensure they are safe. If the risk level is minimal, take some time to consider the consequences before you blow your top.

I am a big fan of direct conversations, I don't think that keeping secrets from each other or dancing around the subject is ever a good idea. However, there will be some instances that it seems like you are just not getting through to your teen, especially if it is a subject they don't want your opinion on or simply because, as we have already established, they pretty much think you are stupid.

My mum used to use the phrase, "You think I came down with the last rain shower", and honestly I did. I genuinely felt at times, like she couldn't possibly understand what I was going through and I certainly felt like I could pull the wool over her eyes. I was invincible. No, I wasn't, she knew exactly what my game was, at least 90% of the time. That other 10% though, that was golden.

If you don't want to show your hand, a useful way to communicate how actions lead to consequences is to tell a story.

Consider, for example, that you discover via your teens messages, that a friend of theirs has been shoplifting. Maybe they stole a can of drink. Your teen hasn't played a part in it, and you know if you speak to them directly you will be told that you have been snooping around. Maybe it's not worth bringing up. Equally, you want your teen to recognise that whilst it may start as a canned drink, it could escalate, or it could end up with others getting wrapped up in it.

So you make up a story. Get your creative juices going and create a similar scenario.

Maybe, "Harriet at work has just been caught stealing. It was really embarrassing for her. She said it just started with taking some stationery, but then as she got away with it she started taking more and more. In the end she stole a Macbook. She's been caught, lost her job and the police have had to be involved. Tut, such a shame. She had so much potential. Poor ol' Harriet."

Admittedly, it's not creatively brilliant but you get the gist, actions lead to consequences. Bad choices can escalate.

The thing is, if you have this chat with your teen, out of the blue, they are going to smell it a mile off. Smart teens, remember.

So instead, have the chat with a partner or a friend, within earshot of your teen. They will connect the similarities between the stories and consider the consequences, without you needing to wade in at all.

Just maybe keep them away from Harriet at your next work event.

> **"I fully enjoy having teenagers. I want them to enjoy the freedom of no responsibility for as long as possible, as you are an adult for a really long time."**
>
> **AROUND THE TABLE**

It's not narcissism, is it?

At around 11 years old, children can experience adolescent egocentrism. Whilst there is light and shade to it, you already know what I am talking about don't you? It gives them "the world revolves around me" vibes. It's not the easiest to live with, for sure, but it's a normal part of growing up, mastering your individualism and finding your identity.

Since the idea of this book rose, I have found myself unashamedly eavesdropping into the conversations being held by teenagers. Although in truth, I use the word conversation loosely.

What I actually usually witness is an exchange between two young people, talking about themselves. Often this plays out over the top of one another, voices rising to be heard above their peers, as they discuss, nay, project whatever is on their mind. And it's fast paced to say the least, not dissimilar to the flow of social feeds they are consuming. It seems to me that their brains are moving faster than ever, skipping from one thing to another. This of course is a generalisation. I am quite sure many teenagers are well versed in the art of conversation, but as digital interactions form the large majority of teenage communication nowadays, I wonder if many have never, in fact, been taught how to converse. It leaves me wondering if in fact, it is a skill acquired from observation, rather than something that is spelt out to us during our youth. Has the opportunity to watch conversations in full flow dried up for this most recent cohort of teens? How many children and teenagers are now growing up watching their parents and others around them, communicating primarily over texts, memes and social media commentary, rather than in person?

During a recent holiday, my husband drew our attention to the amount of people around us, out for dinner with family and on dates, that spent most of the time on their smartphones. To be clear this was not just children or teens, who often get a bad rap for using their phones too much. In fact, on more than one occasion we saw parents transfixed by their phones, whilst their children chatted to one another or ran around the table.

Just to be clear we are not the perfect family. This observation was not a result of superiority, it was more an exercise of a continued justification, to our children, as to why we have always enforced a no phone rule at the table, wherever we are.

Seriously though, once we noticed the level of phone usage in restaurants it became a bit of a game. Enter nature show voiceover, "Here we see a human, in the wild. Easy to spot thanks to the isolated nature, and hunched appearance. You will be able to sidle up and observe this particular creature from a matter of feet, without them even realising you are watching them, all thanks to the unit they hold in their hand devouring their full attention." With phones becoming the most interesting thing in the room, is it any wonder we are losing our ability to converse with each other?

> ❝ **Take care what technologies** ❞
> **you use, because your**
> **consciousness will, over time,**
> **come to be shaped like those**
> **technologies.**
> **- Johann Hari**
>   **Stolen Focus, Why you can't pay attention**

Dear teen,

Imagine a conversation is like adding stepping stones to a river. You and a friend each have a rucksack, full of large round stones to place into the water to allow you to cross.

You reach into your friend's bag for one, as they cannot reach their own, and pass them the first stone to lay. This is representative of asking them a question or inviting them to talk.

They take and lay the stone, whilst it is in their hands it is your time to just listen. Take time to observe the stone being laid.

Then, you step onto this stone together, this is a time to talk together collaboratively and listen to one another in a balanced way. You don't want to fall in the river after all. If you have another question or direction of conversation for your friend, you take another stone from their bag and the process repeats.

If, however, they have something to ask of you, they take a stone from your bag, and hand it to you. I am sure you get the idea now, you have an opportunity to talk whilst the stone is in your hands. You then move together to the next stone for another moment to both talk and listen.

Whilst you can lay a few stones at a time from either bag, it is important by the end to have distributed stones from each bag, in order to reach the opposite river bank.

Note that you are never holding your own stone, before the other person has finished talking, or else you would be unable to listen and the path would not go in the right direction.

Once you have crossed the river, the path remains, meaning if you ever want to revisit a stone together you can.

Positive affirmations made easy(ish)

We got into the habit, when our children were younger, of asking "What did you do well today" to each of us, while eating dinner.

It's something we still try to do, albeit the answers have changed somewhat over the years. It used to be all "I drawed a picture of a horse with a hat on" and now it's closer to "I completed the entire series of Friends...again".

It's a way of starting a conversation that gives insight into your teen's day, and for them too, gives some insight into yours.

You simply move around in a circle and each person delivers something they have done well today, not forgetting the adults. You don't need to explain or elaborate unless you want to. The answer could be simply "I had a really good maths lesson" or "I helped a friend" or even "I made time for myself".

It's tough to start with, whilst it is easy to give praise to others, it can be hard to talk about yourself in a positive light without cringing or being self-deprecating in the process. But with practice it becomes easier. This is an exercise all about creating good habits to support your teens wellbeing, something they can keep.

This tool has a few benefits. It works as a conversation starter, as although you don't have to elaborate, often people will, meaning you may get a little more than the average grunts and 'one worders' for a change. Yippee.

It also gives you a little insight into what your teen has been doing throughout the day, giving you a little fodder to spark up a new conversation at a later time, "Oh you mentioned you helped a friend out yesterday, is everything ok now?"

Lastly and maybe most importantly, these little moments of self (and collective) praise help to lift everyone's spirits and may even provide valuable psychological effects.

According to a study by G.L Cohen and D.K Sherman (2014. The psychology of change, self-affirmation and social psychological intervention) there is evidence to support that regular self-affirmation can improve education, health, and relationships, forming benefits that sometimes persist for months, years even. Self-affirmation is thought to help maintain self-integrity, which is a vital part of managing stressful situations.

Next time you are around the dinner table together, or in the car, why not try it.

"What did you do well today?" - cue grunting.

THOUGHT

I have been wondering if "be careful" is redundant.

It is not specific enough to be useful, it places the thought of fear in our mind before there is anything to be scared of, and it leaves way too much wiggle room to find teenage sized loopholes.

Mistakes were made? Cool

People make mistakes all the time. Daily even.

Teens seemingly make more mistakes than most, can you remember some of yours?

For me they mostly began with getting an older boy to buy us alcohol at the age of 13, that myself and friends would consume at the local park, without our parents knowing. In fact, reading this is probably the first my parents will know about said (repeated) offence. In any case, it was a regular occurrence on a Friday night. We would drink cider often until some of us were sick, and then we would wander home. (Yes that is indeed within the 10% aforementioned).

There was one weekend I didn't attend, one of the teens drank way too much. Long story short they required emergency assistance, but in the first instance, no one dared call anyone for fear of getting into trouble. Luckily, someone came to their senses and an ambulance was summoned. Following medical intervention, they were fortunately ok.

Testing boundaries and discovering their own identity can lead to teens making their own choices and relying on their peers for advice, over their parents or other adults. That means they are less likely to get it right, as they lack experience.

We need to consider the way we treat our teens when they come to us having made mistakes, as they will take this as a marker of how we would deal with any onward mistakes too, however big or catastrophic they are.

> **"It is important not to always do everything for them, I think in this world we often try to protect our kids, but I think it's really good for them that they have to learn for themselves and make mistakes. Even though as parents we don't want them to be sad, make mistakes or go through any adversities, I think that building up that resilience is really important. We have to let them fail in some things for them to grow. That as a parent, has been a huge learning curve."**
>
> **AROUND THE TABLE**

Whenever your teen comes to you with a problem or admission of a mistake, stay calm.

Firstly, be sure to thank them for coming to talk to you about it, even if your first reaction is to lose your shit. Offering a thank you is a leveller. Just listen to them fully before you respond. Hold space for them, no matter what they have asked, done or referred to.

The message always needs to be, I love and accept you regardless, I hear you. After all, don't we all need that? Now that isn't to say there will never be consequences for actions, but responding like this initially, allows time for you to process the situation fully and prevents overreactions.

By forming open channels of communication with your child, they are more likely to approach you with a "this thing happened" or "I have to tell you something".

No matter what it is, they need to know that they can come to you.

If you instead chose to overreact, punish or disregard them without the facts or listening fully, why would they choose to come back to you next time? They won't. They will internalise and keep secrets.

Set a good example when it comes to your own mistakes too. Take them as your own. Admit and cherish them. No one can use your mistake against you, providing you have freely acknowledged it. It can be useful to discuss your own past mistakes with your teen too, depending on how brave or candid you are feeling. There is something powerful about sharing your vulnerabilities, it helps to bridge the gap between "My parents never understand me" to " "Oh, turns out my parents are human after all."

Dear teen,

The only person you should be trying to impress every day is <u>you</u>.

Dealing with peer pressure can be tough but, here's the thing:

- You do have control over how you deal with it.
- You do have control over not bending to peer pressure.

Honouring failure

Innovation always requires failure. More than accepting our mistakes, it's important to acknowledge that without them, we cannot grow. Many tales of success have been built on a foundation of failure.

James Dyson created 5,126 prototypes before finalising his product. The name WD40 honours the fact that it took 40 attempts to get the famous formula right. Henry Ford's first two businesses failed. Albert Einstein and Oprah both had their fair share of setbacks too, through a combination of their own mistakes and the lack of belief from others. Heck, it has even been cited that Walt Disney was fired from an early job, as his boss felt he lacked creativity.

Acknowledging your failures is just as important as celebrating your successes, particularly around your teens. By openly discussing what has gone wrong for you, it allows for your children to see how you have dealt with it. It broadens their comfort zones and allows them to learn from your mistakes as well as knowing how to manage their own. If we step in every time something goes wrong, it allows no space to problem solve or build resilience, after all if we continually rescue them, that is the only pattern they will learn.

If you have not seen it already, the men's mountain biking gold medal victory, claimed by Tom Pidcock in Paris 2024, is well worth a watch alongside your teens.

It is the perfect illustration of not letting a failure affect your progress. It's also a nail biting and exhilarating race to boot. Defending his title and sitting lead, Pidcock suffered a devastating puncture on lap 4, cutting him adrift from the leader of the race, by a whopping 40 seconds. Did he lose his head? Absolutely not.

He stayed composed and calm, taking the opportunity to have a drink of water, whilst the wheel was quickly changed. Unbelievably, he went on to regain his position, taking the gold. When asked about his experience and his unusually calm stature, he simply replied "What's the point in stressing? I have had enough stress this week".

Did you know that many top athletes actually visualise failure and overcoming it? That way, if and when the situation of a mistake or setback occurs, they can deal with it, as they feel like they have already experienced it and still succeeded.

At 13

" You are not weak. You just haven't trained yet.
You can train to be strong.
You can learn to be confident.
You can work to be successful.
And your only limit will be when you decide to stop.

As counterintuitive as it sounds, just as you may have introduced "What did you do well today?" to your family chats, try adding, "What did you fail at this week?" into the mix.

It is interesting to drop at the dinner table. You will likely be greeted with looks of confusion. Have you finally lost it?

Not at all. The fact is the more we discuss, and further than that celebrate our failures, the more we will grow. It is worth noting too, that as your teens become comfortable in discussing their failures, and yours too, there will naturally be less shame within the family environment and beyond.

By taking on your failures and acknowledging them, the fear drops away and you build resilience. You are more inclined to try new things and take chances. If you fall in the future, you will be quicker to get back up again if you are not dwelling on the failure.

> **❝ I've missed more than 9,000 ❞ shots in my career. I've lost almost 300 games. Twenty-six times I've been trusted to take the game-winning shot and missed. I've failed over and over and over again in my life. And that is why I succeed.**
> - Michael Jordan, Failure (1997)

The ritual of eating together

Most people wish they had more family dinners.

According to the February 2021 study "The Benefits of the Family Table" by the American College of Pediatricians, family time at the dinner table has declined by more than 30%. A UK report from supermarket giant, Sainsbury's, of the same year, would seem to support those figures too, reporting that just 28% of households are sharing the same meal in the evening.

The Sainsbury's poll of 2,000 UK respondents found that a busy schedule is the most common reason families don't dine together, with 55% of the population admitting to struggling to find the time. Almost a quarter (23%) of parents stated that their children eat meals in front of the TV or whilst playing on a games console.

Within "The Benefits of the Family Table" study, the majority of parents placed a high value on family meals, ranking them above holidays, play and religious services in helping them to connect with one another. Studies have found that benefits such as maintenance of normal body weight, healthy eating patterns and less disordered eating, are found when families eat at least three meals per week together. Teens having frequent family dinners are more likely to report having excellent relationships with their family.

From the study it seems like there are a myriad of benefits for eating together including improved academic performance, improved family relationships, improved nutrition, a decreased risk of drug, alcohol and nicotine use along with improved emotional wellbeing.

Parents also benefit from family meals, with the study indicating that both mothers and fathers who had more frequent family meals, were less likely to describe depressive symptoms, had a lower stress index, and had greater self-esteem. Yay for us.

As an added bonus, meal times together naturally decreases screen time, for all of us. Win win.

What don't your parents understand about you?
❝ That I just want to have fun all the time.

That is seemingly a lot of benefits from a simple measure, but in the real world it is not always that easy, is it? Between extended hours at work, after school clubs and general teen disdain it can be hard to find the time to all eat together, and when you do, you are likely exhausted meaning slumping in front of the TV is pretty appealing, compared to sitting up at the table, right? For that matter, you may not even have a table. That's ok.

The goal is not to have a 'Darling Buds of May" style dinner. For those too young to catch this reference, the show featured Pam Ferris as 'Ma Larkin' who was continually cooking enormous feasts for her family and friends. This, in today's world, would simply add more pressure to everyone involved. Instead, keep it realistic. Try to sit down together, wherever that may be, 2-3 times a week, or just as much as you can manage. It doesn't need to be a fancy affair either, a quick stir fry, a freezer meal or fish 'n' chips. Just put your phones away and sit your bums down together.

Of course there will be weeks, or longer periods of time where this just can't work. There will be weeks that your teen doesn't want to join you at the table or that fixtures clash. The key is to not allow that inconsistency to become the reality. Keep looping back to it.

How to create a beneficial space for eating together:

- Discuss as a family what nights are best for family meal time, and prioritise it. Add it to a shared calendar and try to avoid booking things during family meal time wherever possible.

- Keep showing up. Keep coming back to that table, even if that table is actually a sofa, and even if there are only two of you at home that evening. They may not be babies anymore, but your teens still require consistency and familiarity.

- If you don't have a table that's not a problem. Just be sure to all sit in the same room.

- Make it collaborative. Encourage your teens to be a part of the meal preparation. Hell, they can cook if they want, it will save you a job after all. Try sticking on their favourite tunes to make it a more inviting environment.

- Create a setting of open conversation, maybe try "What did you do well today" as a starter.

- Shut out distractions. No television, phones, headphones, working or reading.

- Make it clear from the offset that there is a requirement for all to stay at the table until everyone is finished. My children have joked about this rule, as my husband is quite possibly the slowest eater in the entire world. Come to think of it, I wonder if he has crafted that skill, to get them to hang around longer.

Picking your battles

There will always be something. Something that is pissing you off about your teenager.

It could be small, like items left on the worktop instead of being put in the dishwasher. Or bigger, like you have found a stash of alcohol in their room.

Surprising as it may seem, teenagers don't go out of their way to piss us off. In fact, thanks to adolescent egocentrism, they probably don't even spare you a thought most of the time. Ouch.

> "Hormones are clearly hitting at the moment but my daughter is quite a closed person. I have had to learn how and when to approach things with her."
>
> **AROUND THE TABLE**

Whatever the issue, if you need it, take time to calm down before talking to your teen.

- Consider, does whatever you are frustrated about need to be discussed immediately or can it wait until the next family meeting?

- Was there a clear boundary or expectation in place before this incident, would your teen have known that it was not acceptable?

- Does it even matter that much, or can you take the high road on this occasion. For example, if your teen has gifted you one of those delightful eye rolls, maybe try ignoring it rather than allowing it to escalate.

- Have you worked out what you require the outcome to be, is it that you just want the bloody bowl put into the dishwasher, or is there a consequence to the misdemeanour. If the latter is the case, deliver this calmly and keep the level of discipline, in balance with the issue.

If seeing yet another bowl on the worktop tips you over the edge and you happen to lose your shit, be sure to apologise for the overreaction. We all do it sometimes, just as our teens do, but owning your mistake shows humility and provides a good role model for them to learn from.

Do a quick, honest report in your head of the conversations you have had with your teen over the past week. Have there been more positive or negative interactions?

Even though they are growing up fast, your teen still needs praise, we all do. It helps to cement their sense of self-worth and creates a more positive environment all round.

Have a go at consciously and directly delivering praise or compliments to your teen this week wherever you can. Do it without sarcasm or indirect criticism.

For example:

"Thanks for getting to the pick up point on time. I appreciated it" rather than "Thanks for getting to the pick up point on time, unlike last week"

"Good job putting your bowl straight into the dishwasher" not "Good job putting your bowl straight into the dishwasher, mind you it's about time!"

"You smell nice" not "Wow, had that shower at last I see'.

Be a fountain, not a drain.

> # At 13 " Being a tall, athletic woman will one day be your superpower.

Family meetings

Regular family meetings are golden. Get in your favourite snacks, and enjoy ripping each other to shreds for 40 minutes. Joke. Well I was serious about the snacks, and the shredding depends on how the previous month has panned out.

If you want to try this, schedule the meetings monthly and make sure everyone knows it's coming up, so that they have time to consider anything they would like to bring to the table. Allow everyone time to have space to be heard, to bring to the table anything that's not sitting quite right within your family dynamic whether it's a lack of toilet roll replenishment that is grinding your gears or a request for an extended curfew. Most of the time, there won't be too much to say, but by showing commitment to this time to share with one another, the hope is that if and when there are bigger discussions needed in the future, you have already set up a forum to allow your teens to speak up.

It is not quite taking stick territory, but the idea is that everyone gets a fair chance to speak without being interrupted, before others are then able to give their own viewpoint on the matter. Try to steer the meeting to keep it balanced between the general household moans and positive feedback for one another. Make notes of positive things you notice throughout the month and raise them. It's a great chance to celebrate one another too.

Any action points should be written down and stuck somewhere (no not there) to ensure that they are resolved in good time, but certainly prior to the next meeting.

The whole truth

Now this one is controversial. Further to full family meetings, I have recently been trialling 'parental appraisals'. I have held these on a one-to-one basis with my teens.

Asking for trouble, yes maybe. But it seems to have worked pretty well so far.

I learnt about it from a friend, it needn't be a fancy affair, just a little sit down together. It can be in the car, if that's a good place to work it into your day, or maybe sitting having a cuppa together.

Just like in a work appraisal, together you talk about what you, as the parent, could have done better recently, what they think would make you a better parent overall and how certain situations have made them feel.

For us, we always kick off with negative feedback about me and my parenting. Eeep. It can be pretty brutal to hear it from their mouths, comments such as "You made me feel embarrassed in front of a friend" cut deeper than you would expect.

We are all friends here, so let me share a couple of my glowing reports:

"You blamed me for something that was my friend's fault."
"You expect me to speak to the teachers but you just have no idea how it actually is at school."

It's not a tit-for-tat session though, this is about me calmly and fully listening to them, one on one. No offering up excuses or reasons. Just listening. Teens need to be seen and heard, just like we all do. I always thank them for the feedback.

Crucially this technique is not about being directed and governed by our teenagers, it's not a route to allow them to be in charge of our household decisions. You are still in charge because you are the parent, that said, no matter what job you are in it is good to get some feedback from your colleagues sometimes. For the record, I also try to encourage some positive feedback, so I don't leave completely bruised.

For us, I'd estimate a good 75%* of their feedback has been really valuable to me, and it has all been good for them to get off of their chests in a calm manner. That's a pretty good return on investment in anyone's book.

Personally I appreciate this approach as it offers a great platform to teach the art of negotiation and helps when giving constructive feedback. Skills for life.

*The remaining 25% of requests are mainly asking for additional snacks, more pocket money, less singing from me when they are on calls, no chores and later bedtimes. Which are clearly all non-negotiables, especially the singing, right?

> **At 13** " Ignore them. You're beautiful.

Scroll less. Read more

Interestingly, it has been said that reading to your children when they are young could improve their empathy levels, those that continue to read fiction as they grow older are able to more easily access and show empathy. Published by Oatley K (2002) in the study *Emotions and the story world of fiction* it was shown that fiction offers a simulation of social experiences, in which people practice and enhance their interpersonal skills.

> **At 13** " You are capable of so much more than you've ever dreamed of.

Balancing the load

> "I was happy when they became older, and started taking care of themselves more. It's one less thing for me to worry about. Obviously you have different concerns for them but now is the time for them to come into themselves and I enjoy watching their different personalities develop. I mean sometimes it's painful, but I mostly like seeing them navigate the world."
>
> **AROUND THE TABLE**

It could be the fact that they leave empty boxes in the cupboard after eating snacks.

It could be that the worktops are never clear of spilt cereal or milk.

It could be that no matter how many times you ask, there are single, worn socks left around the house.

It could be that the stairs are, quite frankly, covered in shit, long past the hope of ever getting returned to their bedroom.

"Perfect home" influencers have a lot to answer for. It's just another stick for us to beat ourselves with, another comparison to be made against our abilities as a parent.

Well of course I have time to bring up my children, ensure they are all wearing coordinating (and stain free!) outfits, maintain a spotless house that smells like the season, make smoothie bowls for breakfast and 'chop' my cushions. Do you not?

A clean house is not the priority.

That said, there are some jobs which we just can't avoid. Washing, putting out the bins, clearing up after dinner and feeding pets.

But, even if you are Mrs Hinch, these jobs shouldn't all fall to one parent. Particularly if your children are of the not so young variety, I'm looking at you teens.

I can't tell you the best way to manage the chores in your house, it's an individual choice from family to family, but I do know that by sharing the load it becomes a whole lot easier for everyone involved, as it gives a sense of responsibility to all and generally frees up a bit of time, you can use to spend together (or you could just hide out on your own and eat snacks in the time you gain, should you prefer).

The way we work it, is that we have a list of 'family jobs'.

These are functional, base level jobs that we need to do in order to keep our family life running smoothly. They have been clearly communicated during a group discussion and decided on by all members of the family, who live in the house and benefit from said jobs being completed. For us, money never trades hands for the undertaking of these roles.

We have discussed the value of our time, and how it is important to all be adding some of this time into the family pot, so that one person is not taking all of the weight. Of course, if someone is working late, studying for a test or is under the weather then one of us will step in to cover them.

Ours are simple things like the emptying and reloading of the dishwasher, refilling toilet rolls in the bathroom, doing the laundry, emptying the bins and hoovering. Now my children are older, they have picked a few jobs each from our expectation list and they are responsible for those, without negotiation. If they want to opt out from the collective duties, they can, by swapping with someone else for their job. If they shirk their duties, then that's just fine, but... they can also expect to no longer be included in the jobs being carried out by others on their behalf. This could include lifts to see friends or having their washing done for them. In this case they would need to arrange that for themselves. For us the team element has worked really well, and hasn't seen much opposition, although it has taken a lot of consistency to run smoothly.

In addition we keep a list of 'extra jobs', these are roles we could pay to have completed should we choose to, such as washing the car, mowing the lawn and cleaning the windows. For full transparency, I don't pay for the windows to be cleaned, they are actually embarrassingly filthy.

These jobs have all been allocated a fixed or hourly rate, and the teens can choose to undertake them if they want to earn some cash, they just have to flag it up prior to starting.

I am not saying this is the perfect way to manage it, but it works for us and helps to keep the day to day jobs balanced between us all.

Overall the whole family is asked to be mindful of their footprint. I am aware that sounds a little fluffy or idealistic, but it has helped our teens to visualise the issue. There was a stage, where every single room I entered, I was greeted with an echo of who has been doing what there.

Clothes, food bowls, disregarded hair from a hairbrush, squash with the lid off, squeezed teabags on the counter, cupboards open. A footprint left behind, for me to clear up. And that was just my husband.

It's important to recognise that communal areas are not mine alone, particularly as the children grow, I cannot just banish every part of them to their rooms, they need space elsewhere in the home, after all, it belongs to all of us. But, as such, we have to all recognise that these shared spaces are just that, shared. A good rule to live by is to always leave things a little better than you found them. Of course, it doesn't always work out like that, I currently have around 42 pairs of shoes at the front door it seems, but we try.

Taking up space

If I am honest, I have found the interruption of 'adult space' one of the hardest adjustments as my children have grown. Teens going to bed later means less time for myself, and for my marriage. Myself and my husband definitely find it harder to find time for ourselves since teens have arrived into our world. The shift from child to teen creates a loss of space, both physically around the home and mentally, even when they are not there. That can prove to be a challenge.

Teenagers do demand a lot from their parents, they spend more time in communal areas, fill your time with requests to see friends, stay up longer, seem to snack continuously, are more integrated with your decision making and conversations and often demand more of your time emotionally (even if they don't admit that they need you).

I don't have a solution for that I'm afraid, just a nod towards it, in solidarity. Know that if you are feeling squeezed, I see you. I'm squeezed too.

> ## At 13
>
> " I wish that I had known that things that you believe are the be all and end all, they are not. All these moments are fleeting.

"I do remember having a conversation with a friend when my children were quite young, that teens can end up being quite, um, challenging. She said how it was a way of actually making you feel a lot better about it when they move out of home. And I thought that was quite funny at the time, but having experienced it I wonder now if that is the case."

AROUND THE TABLE

THOUGHT

I used to read a book called 'A Squash and a Squeeze' by Julia Donaldson to my children when they were young. You may be familiar with it. It centred around an old lady who felt her house was too small. A 'wise old man' suggested she bring in her hen, followed by her goat, her pig and finally her cow. As you would imagine, it really is a squeeze by the time everything is crammed in. At the point of bursting she is encouraged to "take them all out" and her house suddenly feels enormous. I suspect one day I will find myself wishing that my own house felt small again. Right now though, can someone please take the bloody cow out.

Families that play together

When you think of play, what does that word conjure up for you? Mess maybe? (Eurgh slime). Playing shops, plastic bricks, going to the park?

As your child reaches their teens, the amount of time dedicated to play will have decreased exponentially. In fact, should you have the audacity to mention "going to play" to them, it is likely you will be thanked with a look of total disdain, or at the very least a strong eye roll.

Now, to be clear this is not all their fault. The generation of young people we have before us, have maybe not had the opportunity to play in the same physical way that generations before did. If you mention the game of 'conkers', there is a whole ream of young people that have no clue what it is (because, health and safety).

Teenage play has been impacted hugely by the growth of technology, primarily phone usage. More and more teens are choosing to chat over messaging services or are gaming online, rather than meeting up in person. Bike usage has reduced across the globe, youth centres have closed and parents seem to consider the world to be overall a more dangerous place to be.

Adult play (no smut please), on the other hand, is growing, with more card and board games aimed at adults, escape rooms, murder mystery and interactive dining experiences all seemingly becoming the norm.

When our children are young, we know that play is a vital part of their development. We often encourage role play, building, making and just running off steam. Play encourages creativity, supports cognitive development and improves physical fitness. It helps us to connect with others and learn about ourselves. As we get older, play still makes up a vital part of stress management.

Of course, as we change, our approach to play does too, it is less about the water and sand tables and more about structured, organised activities. This could be sport, crafting, playing cards or hanging out with friends.

The key is finding something that allows you to explore your curiosity, filling your time with something that brings you joy. We need to all be taking play seriously.

Play should always be a priority. It is not selfish, silly or pointless.

> ** We don't stop playing because we grow old; we grow old because we stop playing.**
> **- George Bernard Shaw.**

So go find something fun to do. Drag your eye rolling, reluctant teen along too. The more we show that play in adulthood is the norm, the more they are likely to relax into it for themselves.

Dear teen,

I see you in this crossover. It's not easy, is it.

Right now your life feels like a cement mixer, full of all the things that have come before and all that are ahead.

If you peer in, you'd see childhood toys, memories and moments. It used to be just these. Hugs with your parents, playing in the park, the joy of going to a toy shop, meeting new friends, LEGO®. Every day your mixer would produce the day's cement, something for you to build your day on. Maybe you knew where you stood with that mix. It was playful, straightforward and known. Even if some days were not easy, they were familiar.

Now you peer into the mixer and see new things, hormones, school pressures, peers, new hobbies, the unknown. Every day your mix arrives, to set you up for the day.

Sometimes it's straightforward and easy to understand, full of the confident new teen version of yourself. Other days it's messy and confusing. Memories from before, an argument with your friend and a rogue chunk of LEGO®. That reminds you how it was. Oh, on these days how you wish it was ok to just play with your toys again. On days like this it is hard, it's confusing.

But you should know, my mixer is now at the point of churning out a pretty stable mix most days, if you need some of my mix to help support yours, I am here. Equally, if you need a safe space to drag your childhood toys out and play, I would love to join you. And I promise to not mention it to your mates.

Body language

It is natural for teens to feel uncomfortable in their own skin, after all they are changing so rapidly. The way they look, sound and even the way they smell is constantly evolving. That can feel daunting and uncomfortable.

Rather than commenting on their changing body shape, whether positive or negative, compliment them instead for attributes that are not physical, such as their strength of character, determination or personality. Talk about how the media only ever shows us part of the story and educate them on the pitfalls of following trends and bowing to peer pressure.

Focus on offering them well rounded nutritional education by modelling healthy behaviours yourself. Eating well, exercising and showing our own bodies respect and love helps to set a good example to our teens.

When it comes to puberty, it is vital to speak openly with your teens as early as possible, about their body and the changes they can expect. It is cited that 1 in 4 girls start their period before being taught about them at school.

In our house, as you have probably already concluded, we talk about ALL things.

I have found the more we talk the less taboo there is. Even my husband blushes less these days.

How you personally approach it will depend on your home, your culture and quite honestly your own confidence, but there are so many ways to access these conversations and they ALL get easier the more often you do it. Just start normalising it.

I don't think my children would take it well if I sat them down to have a big 'chat' so whilst that's an option we have never gone down that route. If you feel you need some support with where to start, I have found the Dr Ranj book, *How to Grow Up and Feel Amazing* really useful. It is primarily aimed at boys but works as a good aid for all.

It can be easy to keep procrastinating, waiting until they are old enough to handle tricky conversations, only to find when they are older, you think you no longer need to talk with them because they already know it all. Spoiler; they don't. Stop holding back or waiting for them to ask the right thing. You have to be brave and go to them with what you know they need.

What did 'teenage you' need more insight or education on? Have you given that to your children?

We have had our most interesting conversations sat in front of the TV, I tend to take the opportunity to discuss those *gasp* scenes in films and utilise news stories to discuss subjects that may otherwise be hard to reach. Yes it totally 'cringes them out', but that's just tough luck. More often than not they are interested, even when they pretend they would rather be gouging their eyes out. Following a particularly steamy scene, I was asked by my teen if I felt sex scenes on TV were a realistic representation of real life sex. It opened up a great opportunity to talk about how sex is portrayed in the media and in porn, compared to real life.

I keep reaffirming that there is no shame in asking questions in the hope that they continue to ask them.

WAP

I was just in that moment, the one we all hit when clearing out a room that has been neglected for too long. That point that you look around and think, why on earth did I start this. Knee-deep in crap and losing the will, when my son, who was around 9 at the time, waded in.

> **At 13** " One day you will wish for the body you now 'hate'.

"Can I ask you something Mama?"

"Of course mate, what's up?" (*smiling though inwardly cursing the timing*).

"What does WAP mean?"

Oh lovely. Cheers for that Cardi B.

To give you some understanding of my chosen response, it is probably helpful to have some context first. From day one, I had decided that whenever our children asked us a question, we would answer fully and honestly. I recognise that approach is not for everyone. When, in the past, I have told other parents of my intentions they often experienced sweaty palms, a light case of hives or the immediate need to inform me that I was 'making a rod for my own back', or 'just wait until they are teenagers' (see horrible teenagers chapter).

Actually, to date, it's worked out pretty well. It's allowed my children to know there is no such thing as a bad, silly or shameful question. Every question is safe to ask within our home.

Don't get me wrong, it had to carry some rules as they got older and their questions bigger (such as knowing what knowledge is not to be shared in the classroom). The WAP question was no different.

If you, like my then 9-year-old, are also in the dark about the meaning, 'WAP' was a particularly explicit song released by Cardi B and Megan Thee Stallion, which hit the charts, gaining notoriety due to its spicy content. And if you don't already know the meaning, it may be time to brace yourself, WAP stands for 'wet-ass pussy'. An interesting concept to explain to my son, I am sure you can imagine.

My approach to these 'I beg your pardon moments', is pretty easy to break down, and it's still the technique I employ now that they are in their teens. This is how I did it with WAP...

1 Don't make assumptions about what they do or do not already know.

In the face of a difficult question I tend to first ask their opinion. It allows me to gauge what they already know and what triggered them to ask the question. It also thankfully gives me time to process what I am going to say.

"Oh that's an interesting question, do you have any thoughts on it already?"

2 Answer questions with facts.

Offer facts, to directly answer the question and allow the

conversation to flow to their pace of curiosity.

"Ahh, they are song lyrics right? The word WAP basically stands for Wet - Pussy."
"I know what a pussy is, it's a girl's parts"
"That's right, it is another word for vulva"
"But why is it wet?"
"If you have a vagina, sometimes it can become lubricated, which is another word for wet"
"Why?"
"To keep it comfortable. That's useful during sex, because sex should always feel good for everyone involved*"·

*My son already knew about sex at this point so I took this conversation as an opportunity to gently expand his understanding of consent. As a side note, he never did ask me about the ass.

3 Allow time for follow on questions to be asked.
"Does that all make sense"
"I have another question"
"Go on"
"How is Spider-Man able to make so much web?"

4 Offer opinion, beliefs and rules last.
Only then, give them any rules or opinions that relate to your personal beliefs, culture or opinions.

5 If you don't know the answers, be honest.
Tell them you will look into it. I seem to know less and less these days, owing to the fact I apparently don't have any 'skibidi rizz'.

Now, I am fully aware that some will say that I shouldn't have been talking about sex with my then 9-year-old. It's a common belief that talking about sex, 'just puts ideas into their head'. In case you haven't already guessed, that's not a belief I personally hold - especially now that my little ones are no longer so little.

The thing is, I would much prefer to be putting facts into my teen's head, rather than allowing someone else to put their own version of a story in there. Wouldn't you?

I would much prefer to have an open conversation and answer their questions directly and honestly, over allowing them to absorb nonsense online, from their peers and from television.

My children are no longer asking me questions about Spider-Man, yet I think it is fair to say that the questions and conversations are more 'interesting' than ever. Truthfully, I find myself being 100% sure of the answers less and less "I'm sorry, body count means what?"

It takes far more work to stay ahead of the game, because it all moves so bloody fast, but I am not going to allow my child to be misinformed or misled just because I am too scared to keep up or have a conversation.

What don't your parents understand about you?

❝ We were around at different years of life, so we can't always relate to the same things.

Curiosity repulsed the cat

There are going to be certain subjects that you need to address, even if your teen has not asked questions about them. I completely understand that there may be personal, cultural and/or religious reasons that you have avoided certain subjects to date, but I strongly believe that as a parent you have a responsibility to cover things, albeit in your own way, rather than relying on your teen to find their own way through them. They are surrounded by noise and opinions, so will come across content whether you discuss it or not. There is no getting away from teen curiosity.

Many are able to access the internet to answer their questions, but this can just lead to more confusion. Out of curiosity, I decided to monitor the journey our teens are led on, when they have simple questions and turn to Google to answer them.

I open my Macbook, settle into my 13-year-old mindset, and type "what is a vagina" into the Google search bar. Spoiler; adult me already knows the answer.

The first result is a pretty scientific explanation, as you would expect. It's in depth though and pretty boring, I am not convinced that a curious teen me would hang around here seeking answers. I scroll a bit. Ahh the 'People also ask' section, that's bound to be useful. It is a section generated by utilising user's previously tracked journeys, from question to click. I skim read a few of the automatically generated suggestions in the hope something will enlighten teen me and answer my initial question.

Curiosity repulsed the cat

There are plenty of pre-written questions for me to select from. Hmm, 'What's the purpose of a vagina?', 'What is a woman's private parts called?', 'What does a vagina look like after birth?' yeah, these could do it.

I click on each question and it supplies a little drop down of additional information. One by one I read the answers. Interesting stuff. As I close the tabs, Google helpfully generates new questions that relate to my initial question. My curiosity takes me onwards. I have so far read three questions, and up pops a new one. 'What is a daddy stitch?'. Teen me has no clue but luckily Google helpfully informs me that this is a procedure after giving birth, that sees additional stitches being added to the vagina, to make it 'tighter' in order to increase male pleasure during sex. 13 year-old me is repulsed. So is adult me. Experiment over. I dread to think what I would have found on social media.

Let's get real. If you don't cover these conversations with your teen, you are not offering them protection. If they do not come to you, they will find the answers elsewhere.

It's time to get your blushes out (nope, that's not a euphemism). That's right, just shake them off. You need to get over the embarrassment. Why? Because if your teen doesn't initiate conversations, you are going to have to pull on your brave pants and open up those lines of communication yourself.

For me the fundamental conversations are around consent, puberty, sex, pleasure, social media/online safety and porn. You need to establish your teens' understanding of these subjects and ensure they know you are there to answer their questions.
No judgement. No assumptions. No shame.

Just talk. Yep, it may be awkward the first time. Maybe it's awkward every time? But who cares.

How to kill someone (no not really, it's about pleasure)

Q: "I caught my teen masturbating. What should I do?"
A: "Apologise and try knocking next time"

Whilst on the subject of open conversation, it seems like the right time to talk about educating pleasure.

I'm not talking sitting with a coffee and a paper on a Sunday morning, although that sounds delightful, I am talking about PLEASURE. Satisfaction. Joy.

I have had this conversation with a few adults, the responses I receive cross a spectrum from sheer horror to awe, passing by amusement and embarrassment enroute.

Isn't it interesting that even mentioning the word pleasure at dinner is more controversial than discussing carrying out the perfect murder.

I am the founder of a fledgling project called The Quash. In a nutshell, The Quash is a community that aims to support parents, caregivers and educators to talk with their children with confidence, navigating their questions about sex, health, relationships and all of those growing up rumours. It centres around a platform that is able to be tailored by parents based on their child's current need and questions. We believe that by educating children wholly, that they will be stronger, happier and safer.

The Quash was born, following an incident at my children's primary school. A football coach, who helped to run my children's PE lessons and school holiday clubs, was convicted following the discovery that he had groomed more than 150 children online, over a 12-year period. My children were not involved. I cannot say for sure, as I know this individual worked very hard to cover up his atrocities, but should he have approached them individually, I hoped their open education surrounding sex would have been enough to support them to recognise that something was very wrong.

Aside from such chilling occurrences, I'm quite frankly terrified for future generations having seen misogynist viewpoints gaining momentum online. There is little being done to counterbalance (or wipe away) fake news and hate speech across the channels that children are regularly viewing. It is far too easy for children to lose themselves within a tunnel of misinformation and overwhelm, even when searching for the most innocent of questions.

Sex education does seem to slowly be undertaking a reform, with the introduction subjects such as sexual harassment and sexual violence, the prevalence of 'deepfakes' as well as miscarriage, menstrual and gynaecological health matters being added to the curriculum here in the UK. I welcome these additions, but I am also conscious that sex education is still treated as taboo. Pleasure still takes a back seat, and yet it is increasingly important to educate young people on the matter as it informs how we teach consent and personal boundaries. It also forms a large part of our own self worth as we grow older, we all deserve pleasure.

In the Netherlands they take a straightforward approach to sex education. Lentekriebels week (which translates as spring itching) takes over schools and all children from 4 years old receive compulsory sex education classes. The lessons focus on respecting each other's boundaries, discuss intimacy, cuddling and promoting loving relationships with others and themselves. Some classrooms are visited by a pregnant woman, or nursing mothers to allow the children to ask questions and indulge their curious natures. It seems to be effective too, as it stands, The Netherlands boasts one of the lowest rates of teenage pregnancy globally.

It may seem like a radical approach, if talking about sex does not come easily in your household, but whether you like it or not, your teens are discussing all matters of subjects with their mates. They are also being subjected to a torrent of content online. But, so often the missing part of the puzzle is pleasure.

> **❛❛ Your pleasure belongs to you, ❜❜**
> **to share or keep as you choose,**
> **to explore or not as you choose,**
> **to embrace or avoid as you**
> **choose.**
> **- Emily Nagoski**

Let me be clear, this is not about giving your teen a step-by-step guide in how to pleasure themselves. It goes way beyond the physical notions, instead focusing on teaching them how to understand their own bodies and minds. To know that their pleasure is not (quite literally) in the hands of someone else, or reliant on porn, or society's expectations.

In order to understand yourself and your boundaries, just like when we play as children, self-pleasure is about discovering your likes and dislikes, what makes you feel good and what does not. It helps us to establish our boundaries. And boundaries help to keep us safe.

How to kill someone (no not really, it's about pleasure)

Realistically, it is likely that you may not even know the answers to these questions for yourself. Afterall, were you taught to prioritise pleasure?
It has been well documented that more teens are turning to porn and social media, in order to research sex. Teens are curious, that's natural. But the information they are able to access at ease is shocking.

According to data from the Children's Commissioner UK report, 10% of children by age 9 have seen pornography, this rises to 27% by age 11 and 50% by age 13.

Let that sink in.

Think parental controls will fix it? Nope. There are unfortunately a couple of flaws in relying on parental controls, firstly most children do not find this content on adult sites. The majority, the report found, was viewed on the platform 'X', formally Twitter (brings a whole new meaning to the new name, doesn't it). This was closely followed by Snapchat, and then Instagram.

If you allow your teen free access to social media, then you need to be fully aware that pornographic content is pretty easy to fall across. It is often hidden in plain site making it really tricky for parents and caregivers, because it's likely not picked up by parental controls.

Worse than that, content considered explicit is being hidden using specific 'NSFW (not safe for work)' hashtags, which are a kind of secret code shared amongst users, making it increasingly difficult for the social platforms police to take down these posts quickly. Or so they lead us to believe. There are suggestions that they in fact are in no rush to remove such financially lucrative content.

Further to this, lots of the children in the Children's Commissioner UK report, did not actively search for pornography or adult content themselves at all, rather they were shown it by a peer or sibling.

Many were then too scared to tell their parents because they thought they would get into trouble.

Whilst porn can offer us, as adults, a place to explore our pleasure, we clearly understand (I hope) that porn is not a reflection of real life. The difference when it comes to teens is that in many cases it is being used as a reference point for what sex actually is and what is expected of them when they first try it. As adults we can freely explore our kinks and watch what makes us feel good, should that be our thing, without considering it to be reality.

The issue with teens using porn as a method to educate themselves, is that they, for the most part have had no other measure of sex or sexual behaviours, aside from the voices of their peers, who too have likely learnt through the same route.

The shocking fact is that the large majority of porn portrays the message that women are objects of pleasure, and whilst there is a shift happening within the industry, there is a huge amount of content out there that glorifies and normalises underage sex, unrealistic body and sexual standards, rough and sadistic play such as choking and ultimately places the male orgasm as the goal. To be clear, this is not just negatively impacting on our girls, but has the potential to distort the viewpoint of all of our teens and influence their behaviour.

It is rare, on mainstream pornsites to find representation of intimacy, sensuality or connection.

Teaching young people about pleasure is not about encouraging them to have sex, it is about giving them the full picture. To give them the chance to make informed decisions and encourage them to listen to their gut. It is a vital tool in teaching consent and sexual communication. It helps to increase their understanding, in turn, I would like to think, allowing them to foster their own opinion rather than performing to societal sexual standards.

Whilst porn is the pinnacle of this narrative, social media, film and TV continues to influence our teens daily.

So let's take a deep breath and teach teens a few simple facts;

- Sex should feel good.

- We can experience sexual pleasure on our own, and that is normal.

- Take time to explore what you like and don't before engaging in sexual activity with someone else.

- Don't rely on porn, your friends or the internet for your sex education.

- When having sex or a sexual experience with a partner it should feel good for you both.

- Sex is not just about hetrosexual intercourse. Oral and anal sex are considered sex too.

- Any form of sexual activity requires clear and enthusiastic consent.

- You should always feel safe - if it feels wrong, it's wrong.

- As your parent, I am always here to answer your questions or pick you up if you feel unsafe.

Dear teen,

No is a full sentence.

Pornanalogy

Your teen has asked what porn is. Here's my guide to explaining it to pre/young teens.

Porn is short for pornography.

It refers to anything printed or videos that show sexual activity.

It is important to remember that porn has been created in the same way that any other film has been.

It is created to appeal to all different types of adult audiences, using actors, production teams, lighting cameras and crews. **It is not real.**

Just as people make films that are different genres, love, horror, crime and even downright weird, porn is also made in different styles and with content that is often based around fantasy.

Porn is not a true reflection of real sex as it tends to be exaggerated.

The main problem with watching porn before you have experienced sex for yourself, is that it is impossible to work out what is normal and fun sexual behaviour and what is not.

Sex with a partner, when you are an adult is fun, but some porn contains acts that are abusive and misogynistic, this means it shows hate and violence towards women. This is not normal or acceptable behaviour.

Just like on a film set, when all is said and done, everyone including the actors is paid for their time and they up and leave.

It is then distributed to audiences online.

The problem is if you always watch a fake, heightened version of sex, you lose perspective on what is real, and you can end up with an unhealthy relationship with sex, which will impact on your relationships in the future.

Dear teen,

Imagine Sex is Sugar.

Each time you watch porn, it is the equivalent of eating 10 white sugar lumps at a time. It is all of the sweetness, with none of the beauty, tenderness or fun of sex with a partner. In fact it may even leave you feeling a bit sick.

One day, you get given the key to the most amazing sweet shop you can imagine. It is full to the brim of delicious sweets, these represent sex with a partner.

The thing is, you have gotten so used to the incredible sweetness of the sugar lumps, that no matter what sweet you try, nothing is quite sweet enough. Even though you know these sweets are more special, more delicate and more exciting, you just can't connect. It all seems a little dull compared to the sugar high you have been having.

The problem is, now when you go back to having the sugar lumps, all you can think of is the sweet shop and you can't help but feel you are missing out.

#IRL

Social media has a nasty habit of tricking our brains into thinking that we have connected with others, when we have not. You see your friend's holiday snaps on Instagram and it's easy to think that you have caught up with them about how their trip was. Missed out on a social event but seen the stream of content from it, thinking back, you could have been there.

It can be hard for our brains to distinguish between reality and imagination, so you may be satisfied that your daily intake of social interactions is enough to maintain your relationships and cover off your need for socialising, but there is a very real human need to actually interact with people face to face. Having these interactions even affects our brain chemicals, which we will discuss shortly.

Now I know we talked about the importance of parental attachment vs peer attachment, and whilst I am trying to remain the main influence in their lives, I do still want my teens to have healthy friendships.

I am not sure if you have struggled with this too, but even though I want to encourage my teens to go out and meet their buds, the chances of them A. Organising it (it is of course considered very cringe for me to reach out to the parents of their peers) or B. Their friends actually being available/allowed to meet in real life, is slim.

Teenage brains develop rapidly, with a kind of brain reorganisation thought to take place as they grow. It is easy to consider the most important and influential time for learning would be early childhood, but there is a hella lot going on through teens years too, a lot of which is focused around processing and learning from social exchanges. I wonder then, if we are to expect to learn from the body language and delicate signs given to us through social, in person interactions, how we can be expected to catch these, if our main connection comes not from real life moments but instead from curated content online.

Could it be that we are missing out by not having the chance to study authenticity and natural reactions. By not being party to those pauses in between conversations and the stolen glances across tables. We are losing the nuance.

It got me thinking about how I can foster these interactions for my teen, in much the same way that I took responsibility to arrange playdates and instil a good understanding of social situations when they were younger. Even though they may not appreciate it right now, the responsibility remains for me to nurture their brain.

For us that looks like encouraging them to place their own restaurant orders, offer an open house in which their friends are always welcome, involving them in social events that include a variety of ages (even when I would much prefer to be letting my hair down, away from the prying eyes and judgement of my teens) and encouraging conversations with staff in shops, public transport and actually pretty much everywhere, much to their occasional horror.

What are you doing to enhance these interactions in your teen's life?

Dear teen,

This life of yours, it is not static.

You are constantly moving and evolving, changing direction and growing.

Your life is not a photograph nor preserved in a moment, it is an intricate tapestry.

A tapestry that is being added to and worked on continually. It could fill a museum.

All of those moments, people, thoughts and feelings, all bound together as you journey. As such, no one moment can ever define who we are.

Don't be fooled into thinking the person you are today is the person you will be tomorrow.

Remember, you have control over what is sewn.

Let sleeping teens lie

What's worse than a 'horrible teenager'? A lazy one of course.

Ask anyone for a typical teenage trait and they will likely say, 'laying in bed all day'.

It turns out though, there may be a very good reason for those hours in bed. According to Bupa, a healthy amount of sleep for a teenager is 8-10 hours, but most don't manage to secure that much.

Now of course there are lots of factors that can impact on your teen's sleeping patterns. Watching TV, gaming or phone usage is high on the reasons for a late night, but so is feeling anxious about the day just passed or the day ahead, squeezing in extracurricular activities after or before school can also reduce available sleeping time.

But, even in an ideal word that would see you restricting phones and devices in the evening and tucking up your teen nice and early, fed, watered and seemingly content (the chance would be a fine thing), the likelihood of them dropping off to the land of nod straight away is slim to none. Why? Because of their circadian rhythm.

If you are not familiar with the notion, in simple terms your circadian rhythm is your body clock. It is tuned into factors concerning your body and external influences, to ensure everything is regulating as it should be over a continuous 24 hour cycle. Most life on our planet runs to the beat of a circadian rhythm, for humans it serves many functions, including regulating our sleep/waking patterns.

During puberty the circadian cycle of your teen will shift. It causes teens to want to naturally fall asleep later than they have done previously, in many cases later than adults naturally want to.

Research has also found that teenagers don't produce melatonin until later at night, compared to younger children and adults. This is the hormone your body produces in response to darkness, it's a trigger that tells your body that it is time to doze off.

So, when you are kicking your teen out of the lounge at 10pm, for some much needed personal space, if you are expecting that they will be straight to sleep you are going to be left disappointed. 10pm to a teenager, will feel like it would for you, being told to go to bed at 7-8pm. Actually, that sounds delightful, but I guess you get the point?

Combine this lack of ability to sleep with the requirement to be up early for school, is it any wonder that many of our teens are sleep deprived? There have been calls for the school day to start later for our teens, following recent research, so it will be interesting to see if society shifts to adapt to this need over the forthcoming years. I for one would appreciate not having to run my teens to the bus stop in the dark.

In the meantime, with sleep deprivation being linked to obesity, depression, concentration difficulties and poor decision making, educating our teens on the importance of sleep is vital.

Sleep has a huge amount of benefits, not just for your teen, but for you too, so here are a few tips to try and maximise your zees.

- Prioritise the importance of sleep within your household. I don't know about you, but I am a much nicer person when I am well rested. Adopt healthy sleeping routines for all.

- Encourage exercise - regular exercise promotes an improved sleep quality and duration.

- Reduce caffeine filled drinks. That's not just tea and coffee, but fizzy drinks and energy drinks too.

- Keep your tummy happy, not too full and not too empty. If a snack is required before bed, opt for a banana or almonds rather than high sugar alternatives.

- No phones for at least an hour before bed, always keep them out of the bedroom. The phones, that is, not the teen.

- Check in with your teen to ensure their sleeping environment is comfortable. Is their bed comfy, is the temperature ok.

- Encourage wind down time in their rooms, without any devices for at least 30 minutes before bed.

The impact of blue light

It is worth noting that melatonin production is also affected by light. In a natural environment your body will produce more melatonin as the sun goes down, easing you into sleep in line with your circadian rhythm.

As I am sure you can imagine, artificial light can have a detrimental effect on melatonin production. Harvard researchers found that while any kind of light can suppress the secretion of melatonin, exposure to blue light at night (which is often omitted by electronic devices such as phones) has a more profound effect than other types. Following an experiment comparing the effects of 6.5 hours of exposure to blue light vs green light of a comparable brightness, it was found that the blue light suppresses melatonin for about twice as long as the green light, shifting circadian rhythms by twice as much. During this study, blue light caused circadian rhythms to move by 3 hours.

> ## At 13
> " Make mistakes, it is how you learn. You don't have to be perfect. You are enough and unique and special.

Unfinished business

> "One minute she was dancing around the kitchen to 'Happy', clapping, smiling and dancing. She knew all the moves. The next thing I knew, she was laying in her bed, refusing to go to school. And I was like, how the hell did I miss that? I was here the whole time and yet I missed it. What happened in between that I just didn't see? It was like someone swapped my child for someone else."
>
> **AROUND THE TABLE**

For me parenting a teen is a constant feeling of pushing and pulling, both within my connection with my teen and internally with myself.

I have raised my children intentionally, with the view that they are their own people and that they need to be independent enough to leave me one day. Honestly though, as we work through these teen years, I don't actually feel ready to let them go quite yet.

I crave days of curling up and reading *The Gruffalo* together, doing silly voices and hearing them giggle. I would love to, just for a moment, go back and have the chance to really pay attention to the way that they would watch my face so intently, as I read. Their little faces transfixed with what was to come, as the little brown mouse explored the forest, despite the fact they had heard the story a hundred times before.

Now, though, it is becoming their turn to explore, yet it is not as clean cut as just letting them go, as they still need me. As the tide runs in and out, so too does their dependence on me.

They move out to explore, but centre back home, out again and back. I guess my role now is to be the beach. Constant and unwavering, supporting them to try, to fail to explore, and allowing them to roll back home whenever they need to. Always being the beach is hard though, isn't it.

It's hard watching them go, especially when it's not always in the right direction. Especially when the sea is full of unknowns. Especially when I am not truly ready to let them go.

Dear teen,

I will always be your beach, underneath your waves.
Roll out to explore who you are and roll back in again.
I know the tide will go out completely one day, and I will wave from the shore.

I will wait it out until the next high tide.

However long it's been. You can always come home.

Is it just getting harder?

I was talking with two friends this morning about our teenagers. Something that the three of us find ourselves discussing on a regular basis.

Shenda has two girls, 6 years apart. Her first born came along when she was just 17 herself, as such, her youngest has just turned 18.

Lisa has a teen too, in the second year of high school.

I remember, clear as day a few years back, standing in my kitchen and Shenda saying, "Ladies, make the most of your little ones. Having a teenager is the hardest thing you will face. I miss mine being young so much." I remember brushing the comment away, getting swept up in the general flow of conversation, but I wish I had asked if she was doing ok. If she needed to talk.

Switch to now and 'teenagers' seem to be our favourite subject.

We second guess our decisions, use each other as soundboards, relay conversations and moments we have had through the week with our teens. We use Shenda's experience to help us to navigate this new terrain, and we do it together. A band of mothers. Without fear of judgement from one another. After all, Shenda warned us this time would come a long time ago, she gave us permission to feel deeply about it, as she did. It feels hard sometimes to have left your little ones behind. And that's ok.

When I talk to those who have brought up teenagers before me, it often leaves me wondering if this whole parenting shebang is getting harder. Is navigating the world of parenting teens more troublesome than it has previously been, or has it always been this way?

The main change of course in the here and now, is that we have the additional territory of social media, phones and the internet in general to work our way through, that parents before us didn't. A barrage of knowledge and standards to uphold. It is fair to say also, we are lacking the community many families need to feel supported, instead most of us are bringing our teens up in nuclear families. More parents are working long hours to cope with financial pressures and our days are scheduled out to the max.
But there have always been challenges. No matter the generation we have lived through. Maybe every generation feels they have it tougher than the one that came before?

"Social media is the biggest change. My eldest's first phone was a Blackberry. It is a totally different world now. Yes she would be calling or texting her friends but the phone wasn't glued to her. She was using MSN and Skype. No apps, no Whatsapp. She could just go to school. It wasn't a constant presence. A lot of my friends are older, and they don't understand it either.

My youngest daughter posts on Tiktok. I follow her. Last week she posted saying "when you feel like the odd one out in your family" so I asked her about it. I said to her "What do you feel like that for? You're not the odd one out" It was my attempt at connecting with her, checking she was ok. She blocked me."

AROUND THE TABLE

But everyone else's parents...

It's a phrase we have all used I am sure. "But everyone else's parents let them..."
Insert, stay out in the dark, have the latest gear, have as much money as they want, watch 18 (R) rated movies, eat sugar until they throw up, go to house parties, use social media.

It's pretty easily navigated with a simple reply of "Well I'm not everyone's parents" is it not? I am joking, of course.

> **"My daughter was an hour and a half late home the other night. I must have called her 100 times. I couldn't get hold of her and all sorts of things were running through my mind. I got myself in a frenzy thinking she was dead. Then she just walks in, like nothing has happened."**
>
> **AROUND THE TABLE**

As an adult you know it is simply not the case that "all parents are allowing something to happen". It could be because you know said parents and are familiar with their take on the situation, maybe because you recognise it is an unrealistic standard, maybe you can see that your teen is just playing all the cards in order to get their desired outcome.

It could be that there are indeed a handful of parents who allow their teenagers to partake in activities that you consider inappropriate for their age, or in truth that other parents are allowing their teenagers to partake in something you are just not comfortable with.

I can't advise on what is wrong or right, as every situation is different. What works for them won't necessarily work for your family. Know that you do not have to change your mind solely based on the behaviours of other parents. What I can suggest is that no matter the situation, you give yourself time.

Time to consider fully what it is your teen is asking. Look at it from a wider angle and consider neutrally, your take on it. Try not to be reactive or allow your own negative experiences to overwhelm your thoughts. Once you have a decision, communicate it fully and honestly to your teenager.

Stay consistent and open in your decision making process. Take other people's opinions into consideration by way of research, if it helps, but do not let those opinions be your sole reason for deciding something.

We often discuss how social media is affecting young people. How it is informing their decisions, guiding their behaviours and impacting on their mental health, and it is, all of those things. What we don't discuss enough yet is how social media affects and informs societal shifts on another level. On a huge scale.
Social media is not just responsible for affecting the lives of children and teens, but adults, just like us too.

Be honest. Have you used social media as a reference point for parenting? Have you compared others to yourself or your children to theirs? Have you wondered how that parent manages to 'do it all'?

Maybe the tables have turned, maybe it is now us, the parents, that are considering the age old "But everyone else's parents let them...". Are we, fueled by what we see online and are absorbing from 'experts', at serious risk of approaching a time where we as parents now think "But everyone else's child does it"?

Comparing yourself or your family to others is a dangerous game. It is important to remember that the 'reality' that we are fed online, is a carefully constructed story. The snapshots we are allowed to see, often make up a tiny part of someone's life, or are in fact fabricated or embellished to give a certain perspective to us, the audience.

When we are not 100% happy with ourselves, be it the way we look, our perceived status or our abilities, it is easy to get pulled into a comparison trap. But I say this as your friend, social media will not make you feel better.

No excuses. Start now...

- Unfollow all accounts that cause you to compare yourself to them.

- Spend less time on social media and more time doing something that makes you feel good.

- Set time limits. Dedicate only short and limited windows throughout the day for social media usage.

- If you find yourself starting to compare yourself to others, remind yourself that you are only seeing the highlights of someone's life. It is an edited version, not a true picture of it.

"I wish I had known that any difficult period will come to an end. Any tough points will come round. It's about keeping communication open at all times. She did have moments when she pushed the boundaries and pushed my buttons of course, but it's also nice to see them evolving and growing up into themselves too."

AROUND THE TABLE

At
13

" You don't have to do any of this. You can just be a child and go outside and play and just be you.

Happy brains

Our brains are complex things, I would not like to state that I am any way qualified to give insight into the intricate workings of our minds.

I have however fallen upon someone more qualified than me. TJ Power is a neuroscientist. I first discovered his work while listening to a podcast and have been fortunate to be able to connect with him since. I have included a snippet of our chat at the end of this section.

Thinking back to when I first listened to TJ talking, it struck me how accessible he made a very complex subject, talking top level brain science, alongside relatable, real time examples and exercises.

Following the podcast episode, I shared my findings with my family by creating an exercise of my own, directly related to TJ's theory and then coercing them all to take part. I want to share it with you, as I think it is really valuable stuff, but first, you will need some context.

Our brains developed thousands of years ago, tailored to allow us to thrive within our environment. But as we all know, this environment has rapidly changed over the years. This has resulted in the chemicals in our brains being thrown out of balance which has been widely cited as the cause of many physiological issues for us as humans, leading to an increase in anxiety, depression and stress. In basic terms, there are four main chemicals within our brains that all play an important part in our happiness and brain health. These are Dopamine, Oxytocin, Serotonin and Endorphins.

TJ's groundbreaking creation of the theory of "The D.O.S.E Effect" centres around a gamified approach to improving our mental health. He believes that we are able to have a reasonable amount of control over these chemicals and in turn, rebalance our brains and return to a less stressed and overall happier state of mind.

Let's explore these chemicals in more detail to understand how we can harness their strength for the benefit of our teen's brains and our own:

Dopamine

Dopamine plays a huge role in our mind's reward system. It helps with our ability to feel pleasure and joy, it was originally dished out to our brains after great moments of effort. Hunter gathers would have to hunt, build and survive - if they succeeded only then would they be rewarded with a hit of dopamine. Thanks to technological advances, we can now easily access dopamine with much less or no effort at all. Doomscrolling for example gives us an easy and fast hit of the chemical, but whilst access to easy dopamine may sound like a win, once we stop scrolling our dopamine levels come crashing down. The problem is, that being in a state of low dopamine tends to make our brains anxious.

Other things that cause an unhealthy boost followed by a rapid drop of dopamine include alcohol, vaping, binge-watching box sets and watching porn. Yep, you read that right, sex should be instinctive and take effort, but watching porn takes no more than a couple of clicks of your phone (or so I am told), so it throws out our dopamine balance and depletes our resources.

Powerful and useful hits of dopamine come not from low-effort, high-reward activities, but instead from high-effort, high-reward activities. Such as cooking, weight lifting, reading and sex (yey).

Oxytocin

Oxytocin is often referred to as the love hormone.

It is released in moments when you feel happy, safe and loved. Vital during childbirth, oxytocin stimulates contractions and the flow of breast milk.

Physical touch, sex, positive social interactions and having a good conversation can all trigger oxytocin to be released. In fact, just seeing, hearing or even smelling your loved ones can give you a boost. Unfortunately I don't think stinky teens count.

Interestingly there is evidence to say that texting a loved one does not release oxytocin but a phone call or a video call does. So switch when you can, and enjoy the rush. Or, as we have previously discussed together, don't text or shout up the stairs to your teen when dinner is ready. Go and collect them in person. Rest your hand on their arm occasionally. Go in for that overdue hug. Be present. It will do you both good.

Serotonin

Serotonin helps to regulate your mood. It plays a part in your appetite, sleep patterns and stress levels. You can naturally boost your serotonin levels by simply doing things that you love. Dancing, listening to your favourite tunes or cooking maybe? Sunshine is also proven to increase your serotonin levels.

Endorphins

Before dopamine took the reins as the most talked about brain hormone endorphins ruled, often talked about after exercise. Endorphins are, as you may already know, released after working out. They are also released when the body is experiencing pain, in order to help alleviate it. Endorphins are a punchy little tool, they can lighten your mood, lower your stress levels and generally give you those feel good vibes.

Of course, you will have worked it out by now that I am no doctor. My version of this exercise, whilst it hasn't been scientifically tested, does work for my family, as a tool to keep us focused on what we should be prioritising (good vibes) and what we should be minimising (screen time for example fuels our anxieties and makes us all less motivated).

Quick disclaimer, everything I have shared here is a reflection of my own understanding and continued personal research. I have delivered it to you here, in basic terms. If you would like to know more, follow TJ's work online or better still, grab a copy of his book. I am sure your mind and that of your teens, will thank you for it.

Pay attention to your brain's hormones with this simple exercise:

- Wrangle your family together (this could admittedly be the toughest step on the list).

- Take an A4 sheet of paper and divide it by four with a large cross.

- In each section write down the names of each of the main hormones and a reminder of each, Dopamine (effort), Oxytocin (love), Serotonin (sunshine and self-care) and Endorphins (physical activity).

- Now consider some things you can do daily that will help you to achieve a healthy hit of the hormones your brain needs, across each of the four sections you have set out. It could be reading (and maybe even completing) a book, partaking in sports, making your bed every morning, spending quality time eating dinner together or heading out on a family date night.

- Make it count. Put up your completed sheet somewhere you can keep an eye on it, as a reminder to do something from each section daily. Remember, this is an activity for you too, not just your teen.

Of course, just like everyone else I have accosted this past year, I couldn't pass by the opportunity to ask TJ a few 'around the table' questions:

NH: What do you think the most important thing is we can do as parents, to support our teen's brains and mental health?
TJ: Utilise their social media feed to identify their number one interest. It will be one of the most frequently occurring videos in the feed. For example cooking, singing, music or art. Then guide them to engage in this activity regularly rather than only watching it.

NH: What did 13-year-old you need to hear?
TJ: To prioritise seeing my friends, to go hiking with them, getting off technology and building my confidence through stepping out of my comfort zone.

NH: Why do we need to pay attention to our brain chemicals?
TJ: They provide the clearest explanation possible as to why the modern world is creating mental health challenges and the most accessible solution to solving this difficulty.

NH: What else do we need to know?
TJ: That the number one priority is learning to physically separate from your phone. The key to breaking the addiction is not always having it next to you in every single moment. The dopaminergic urge for it diminishes if there is distance between you and the device. When you're eating, cooking, walking, socialising, working or watching TV - put the phone far away from you.

STOP

If your teen comes into the room to talk to you or tell you something. Stop. Put down your phone, stop working, pause the TV. Whatever it takes to give them your full attention.

Just be present.

Parenting. It's not all it's cracked up to be

> "I see these gender reveals nowadays on social, and see stories in the press of pregnant celebrities celebrating the fact that they are having a girl, and they will be their 'mini me' or their 'best friend', or that they are having boy and they are looking forward to them playing sports with them or whatever. And I'm thinking, you have no idea. You have no idea what they will be like, who they will become. You have no idea of how hard this can be."
>
> **AROUND THE TABLE**

I don't want to be negative, but I do want to keep it real for a moment.

Parenting, just like many other aspects of life, is sold to us, sugarcoated. The fairytale of becoming a parent, is then reinforced by the perfect highlights we see across social media, the press and closer to home from our friends and family. It is rare that people show their vulnerabilities, worries or struggles about being a parent, as they don't want to come across negatively or look like they are doing a bad job. Worse still, they could look ungrateful.

I think it is ok to look at parenting from an 'also' perspective. Admitting something is hard, does not mean you do not appreciate it. I can love something and also find it a challenge. I can sometimes want time away from my children but I also have days when I miss them not being dependant on me.

I am very, very grateful to have my children. What they have taught me and gifted me, could never have arrived in any other form. I love them more than anything. Also, parenting is harder than I thought it would be in so many ways and I have sometimes lost myself along the way.

The shift between child and teen has been the biggest challenge so far. I am not saying it will take the win for difficulty. Ask me in 10 years... then again in 20.

I also think that it is true that we tend to forget how it really felt in times gone by, romanticising what has been. I remember the cuddles, the giggles and the love of toddlers, but I am pretty sure the memories of sleepless nights, tantrums and soft-play birthday parties have faded somewhat. You remember not being able to sit on the toilet alone?

One thing for sure is that parenting is life changing, it just may not be in the way in which we expect.

> **At 13** " What you are experiencing now will inspire you to happiness and success. You won't feel that right now, but when you do, you will not be defined by the bullies. You will stand up for yourself with pride and self worth.

Play it louder

If it can be a yes, make it one.

If you like the song your teen is blasting out of their room, tell them.

Get them to crank it up.

(Maybe don't use the word crank though, you will risk losing any brownie points you have gained)

Comparison game

The comparison game doesn't just affect our teens.

It can affect us big ass grown-ups too.

Oh, my teen is simply excelling at school.
Oh really, my teen just got offered a place in the under 16s team.
Oh yes, my teen is rocketing through their exam prep.
Check out how mature/loving/funny/confident my teen is.

Well, bravo Claire. Well done on all the amazing parenting and making me feel like I am failing miserably.

During a recent meeting, a mother shuddered and said to me "The best thing about my children becoming teens was that I could step away from all of that unspoken competition that happens between parents".
(Honestly once you are paying attention there are parents seeking solidarity and reassurance everywhere).

If you are still in the thick of it, please don't forget that when you are surrounded by other parents, particularly ones you don't know all that well, real life can become a bit 'Instagram'. You only get to see the highlights.

You don't see the disagreements, the repeated conversations, the behind the scenes angst. You have no idea how many times Claire goes to wipe her bum each week, only to find that the toilet roll has been used and not replaced. You don't have insight into what their relationships with each other are really like, how stressed Claire is feeling at trying to be everywhere at once or how many pairs of socks are left strewn around her house. You certainly shouldn't be tempted to compare yourself to anyone.

Take this as your friendly warning, to shake off the feeling that you are not good enough. Stop comparing yourself to imaginary Claire and focus on yourself.

It got me thinking about how we parent and how our own parents likely steer this whether you want them to or not. If you have had supportive parents, you may try to clone their techniques. If your situation was less than ideal, it is likely you will actively try to parent in a different way to that of your upbringing.

The thing is, everyone and every situation is different. Even if you had a perfect and happy upbringing, even if you applied that same technique to your own children you would be faced with different results. Equally it is worth taking notice of the fact that even if you do make some of the same mistakes that you were subjected to, the way you deal with them will be different. Again resulting in different, hopefully more positive, outcomes.

> **❝ Children are not things to be ❞ molded, but are people to be unfolded**
> **- Jess Lair**

Overall, there are simply too many variables to be able to parent effectively by behaving like someone else. Your teen is unique and so are you, society changes daily. Your situation can never be the same as someone else's, so don't waste time trying to make it so.

The only thing we can do is to try and live and parent as authentic and true versions of ourselves. If you are constantly aiming to be someone you are not, you will fail.

Of course it is sensible to stay open to ideas, suggestions and to be aware of what is going on in the wider world, yet I am certain that there is a benefit to focusing on the work that needs to be done inwardly, within ourselves, before looking outwards. If this was prioritised over trying to measure up to the expectations or the perception that we have of others, would we find ourselves becoming more present as parents? I suspect the answer is yes.

> ## At 13
> " It's all gonna be alright. All of it, all the things that you stay up at night worrying about, all the things that you look in the mirror and fear, they are all going to be alright and you're going to be alright.

Stop taking it so seriously

"It's something that I've only really discovered now that my boys are nearing the end of their teen years, but I wish I'd known how much fun it's going to be. I wish I hadn't taken all of their 'teenage hell' moments so literally and let those moments destroy my own mood at times. I wish I'd realised that these are just phases and that I could have had a more lighthearted approach to some of the moments, rather than me getting all upset and angry and fed up.

I would have loved to have been a bit more stand back knowing it will pass. But I've just caught it. I've caught it at the stage where I realise that it's fun and I realise that the things that they do are actually quite funny. I've tried to find the humour in them, rather than taking everything so personally and getting upset. I've learnt to relax into it and just sort of laugh in the way that you would have when a toddler does something ridiculous. They're managing their hormones so give them a break."

AROUND THE TABLE

127

Over the last few years I have been keeping account of some of the phrases my children have said to me. It started with things like "Next doorbers" instead of next door neighbours and "swirliture" instead of signature. In recent times, things have gotten less cute. I have collected "I'm just going to stay at the rec, surely you have a responsibility to collect me?" and a personal favourite of mine, "I hate picking up peas, it's so stressful".

Disclaimer. I am not suggesting you use this exercise for anything other than keeping your own sanity in check (certainly don't do anything silly like include them in a book).

It's not always easy but if you can, try and tread through the stressful moments with lightness.

There is a practice that you may be familiar with, the 5 by 5 rule. I'm not sure who came up with it, but whilst parenting teens, I thank them for it on a regular basis. When something is stressing you out, or worrying you, take a moment to breathe. Consider if this issue will be something you will still be worrying about in 5 years. If the answer is no then don't allow yourself more than 5 minutes to worry about it, and then move on from it.

If all else fails and the wheels come off, at least you will still have a cracking list of phrases to present them with on their 21st. I jest. No hitting them over the head with their own words.

> **"I always took the side of the school - I always thought it was his fault. On reflection now, I am not so sure."**
>
> **AROUND THE TABLE**

Lessons in acceptance

"I'd rather you than me" that's the usual retort, when Emma explains what she does for a living. We are sitting together at the dinner table, putting the world to rights. Not an unfamiliar scene. Emma is a head of year at a UK high school and we have gotten round to talking about teenage behaviour, it seems to have become somewhat of an obsession of mine, doesn't it.

You can forgive me, given the number of teenagers Emma has under her wing, it would be a missed opportunity not to tap into her knowledge base, on all of our behalf.

"So Em, tell me. If you could give some helpful advice to parents of teens, based on patterns you have seen within school, what would it be?"

"I think the two biggest things that a teen can receive from their parents are acceptance and boundaries. Acceptance and love obviously go together, it is important that teens know that they're accepted for whoever they are and for whatever they like. Just feeling loved, feeling accepted and feeling like that you can go and speak to your parents about whatever you want to speak about, is really important.

Parents also need to be making sure that their teens hear and fully understand what the boundaries are for them, because it'll all be really different between different families. I'd say my own mum was pretty laid back when it came to lots of things, but I knew which things she wouldn't stand for and therefore I didn't really push it in those areas. You know what it's like, we've all been a teen haven't we. You sometimes push your boundaries as much as you can. I think I'm really lucky as I have always felt really accepted and loved by my family, but looking at it from a teacher's perspective, there's lots of children that don't have those things and do find it really hard. When there are no boundaries in place that is when it causes problems that we often see reflected in school."

I wholeheartedly agree with this sentiment.

Our teens do need these things in abundance.

So a challenge for you this week, should you fancy it:

- [ ] Show your teen your love. Tell your teen that you love them not just with your words but with your actions. Set up a spa night for the two of you, spend some time joining them for a game on the computer, drop a little package of sweets or chocolate on their pillow, take them on a date, hug them.

- [ ] Tell them that you are proud of them.

- [ ] Take an interest in what they are doing/watching/who they are talking to.

- [ ] Don't be offended if you are told you are cringe, weird or you are dismissed. Eye-rolls are a sign of progress... or at least that is what I keep telling myself.

The next step, we need to nail down our boundaries.

"I had a very kind of innocent childhood, brought up abroad and then going to boarding school in Ireland. I wasn't really exposed to popular culture. I was really sporty too, so I was quite clean living. I never really got into all the teenage stuff until later, and I was pretty naive about that. I thought my son was like me, but he wasn't, so I wish I had been a bit more conscious of what was actually going on as actually drugs were a big part of school in London. Thankfully my son wasn't attracted to any of the harder drugs which were accessible, but he did smoke skunk and that took its toll on his mental health for sure. He was left to his own devices a lot of the time. Not on his own, but you know, I trusted him. I tried not to rein him in too much like my parents did with me. There were rules, but I was lax. I didn't acknowledge the fact that this new 'skunk' was not the same as the seemingly more innocent type of grass that I used to smoke when I was 18.

It dawned on me, you know, over time when I saw the effect it was having on the guys. By then it was too late. Thank God he had the strength of character to just say to me one day, Mom, I don't want to do this. It frightens me. I don't like the thoughts I'm having. And he stopped, but, you know, it really poisoned him for quite a while. It made him very paranoid and very emotional. If I could go back, I would have been a more present mother. My head was turned. I'd fallen in love. Was he neglected?

I don't think so. He had one parent present all the time, but was it enough, you know? Maybe I'm just feeling guilty."

AROUND THE TABLE

131

Boundaries

You remember when your teens were those little dots, who required consistency and routine in order to learn and get things right? Well from where I am sitting, bringing up teenagers seems to require much of the same level of attention.

I'm not talking helicopter parenting or micromanaging their every move, but I am suggesting that they probably need your support more than they let on.

As we have established, boundaries are helpful for teens. Don't worry, by putting them clearly in place, you will not smother them. It actually appears to have the opposite effect.

By having clear lines of communication and set rules, it gives your teen more independence and allows you to have to step in and discipline them less often. In theory. To be clear, I am not expecting this to be a tool for exemplary behaviour. Let's not kid ourselves hey, I don't imagine you thought it would work that way either.

"Rules are meant to be broken" springs to mind, so what's the point?

Well there's three parts to it as far as I can see.

The first is, it helps you to pick your battles, as we discussed earlier on. If you have established your limits and expectations without emotional charge, you are less likely to make rash decisions. It gives you more of a wide-angled view when you are in deep, trying to navigate an issue. I don't know about you, but I find it pretty hard to make good choices when I am seeing red. You will also have a clearer idea of what 'level' of offence has been caused by the boundary being overstepped, or the rule being broken. That makes way for fairer and more effective consequences.

Secondly, your teen clearly understands what is expected of them. Different families have different rules. For example, imagine whilst at a sleepover, your teen watches an 18 horror film. You are shocked, they shouldn't have done that, but they explain that their friend's parents said it was fine (translated from a shrugged 'whatever' and an explanation into why said friend's mum is way cooler than you).

Now, if you have a *rule* in place that clearly states that they are not allowed to watch anything over a 15, and they know that, then a boundary has been broken. Depending on your parenting style, it's reasonable that this would carry a consequence.

If you just had an *expectation* that they would know that was not acceptable, then they have not broken the rule because there wasn't one. In this case, whilst you can advise your teen that you wouldn't have expected them to watch an 18, it wouldn't be fair to lay down a consequence for this.

Lastly, having some "teen rules" helps you to stay consistent alongside anyone else that you are parenting with, be that a partner you are living with, an ex or other support networks. It keeps you on the same page.

Whatever stage you are at, I suggest sitting down for a bit (with a cuppa of course) to clearly establish your expectations, rules and boundaries. Write them down if that helps. If you parent solo this will help you to stay resolute in your decisions. If you parent alongside someone else, it's a useful tool to see where your viewpoints are on certain matters. It's somewhat of a journey of discovery in itself, to understand where your viewpoints meet, and in fact don't. Myself and my husband have been together for many years, and are generally pretty much aligned when it comes to decision making in life, so I found it surprising where our viewpoints differed at this stage of parenting. We could remember being parented ourselves through our teens and could recall how those decisions panned out and how they made us feel, so I think it caused stronger opinions of what we would like, and what we wouldn't.

I wouldn't recommend drawing on your own experiences wholly, as it can cause you to parent through fear or to live vicariously through your teen. Start from a blank canvas.

Let's start with a common subject to start with. Consider your take on alcohol: which option sounds closest to your approach?

A 0% tolerance approach. No alcohol before the legal age limits, whatever the situation.

B It's fine for my teen to have alcohol, but only a controlled amount and only when they are with me.

C I am happy for my teen to drink. I can't stop them, they will do it anyway.

Then create rules that fit with your own values. If for example you chose option B, what exactly is a controlled amount to you?

Overall, give consideration to your take on:

Alcohol
Drugs
School
Homework
Friends and free time
Exercise and nutrition
Age limits on games, TV and film

House rules and housework
Bedtime
Phone usage
Social media
Sex and relationships
Curfews
Money
Gambling

I have found it really handy having this chat before issues have arisen, which trust me they have, and continue to do so. Giving pre-consideration to these matters allows both me and my husband to be able to make decisions regarding boundaries and behaviours, knowing what the other person considers to be the right (or at least agreed on) approach too. It's a little like having a personalised do's and don't guide, and who doesn't need one of those when it comes to parenting?

Once you have the bones of a plan, you can play these 'do's and don'ts' up against 'feel real scenarios':

What the dickens should we do if teen calls us drunk?
What if we discover teen is having underage sex?
How about if teen has instigated a fight?
What if teen is generally being a mahoosive pain in the... you get the picture.

Then, once you have a guide (of sorts), even if it is just in your mind, use that as a foundation when you are educating your teen about their behaviour. The chances are you won't need to explain every element piece by piece to them, as much of this 'guide' will be formed on top of mantras your family have probably run for years. It will just be those new lessons and those that are adapted with age that will need to be set out for clarity's sake.

Don't be scared to discuss moments when your teen has walked a little too close to the line, or in fact skirted over it, as mine often do. It's your job to walk your own line between being 'Nagatha Christie' and a 'cotton wool wielder'. Go on soldier.

THOUGHT

I know of families who...

- Let their teenagers go wherever they want, whenever they want
- Let their teens drink alcohol freely
- Prioritise school work over socialising
- Allow their teens to vape
- Allow their underage teens to have sex under their roof
- Don't let their teens have a phone
- Don't allow their teens to have sleepovers
- Do not know who their teens are hanging around with
- Don't allow their teens to go out on a Sunday
- Give their teens unlimited funds
- Monitor their teens location via their phone
- Allow their teens to have beauty procedures such as lashes, gel nails and bleached hair
- Restrict their teens from having relationships

Who is right and who is wrong? Is it clear cut?

Popcorn

Choose a family code word and explain to your teens how it can help to keep them safe.

It can be anything you like.

Pick a word together. Anything that stands out enough to be noticed by you, as it wouldn't regularly be used in a conversation, but ensure it is a word that is normal enough to not be noticed easily by others.

This word should be used in any 'come and get me now' situation.

If for example your teen is at a friend's house and something makes them feel uncomfortable or scared, they can use this 'code word' secretly during a call to you.

For example, imagine your word is popcorn and you pick up a call from your teen.

"Hey Dad, I am just at Sam's house. I think you said you are going to the shop today, so I just wondered if you could pick me up some popcorn?"

"Of course I can. I will be there in 10 minutes."

We also have an emergency emoji to enable a quick text, if a call is too obvious for the situation.

Anti-social

> "It's totally different now. I just feel like I don't
> understand it. I am living in a complete tech-gap."
>
> **AROUND THE TABLE**

It has been widely reported that Silicon Valley bosses have imposed strict limits on the tech and online platforms they allow their own children to use, despite being fully responsible for releasing them to everyone else's families, with limited restrictions and certainly no warning labels. It would seem, they are well aware of the addictive nature and dangers that social media poses.

American social psychologist and author of *The Anxious Generation*, Jonathan Hadit, is one of the many experts that have raised concerns around social media and tech usage in, not just our teens, but all of us.

Jonathan cites that the tech companies are to blame for the shift in our society and a marked rise in anxiety, stating "We overprotect children in the real world and underprotect them online".

Having overseen social media advertising for many years as part of my daily role, I have been with Instagram from the start. I do not want to jump on a bandwagon or catastrophise social media as a whole as it can, for some, be a great tool. It can bring connectivity to those who are lonely or unable to see their families on a regular basis, encourage us to step out of our comfort zones, allow us to seek solace and like-minded people or expand professional connections.

I happen to enjoy social media overall. I'm not an 'influencer' so I don't spend time creating content particularly, but I do enjoy documenting moments in my life and spend a lot of time on social media through my work and to aid research, for projects such as this book.

That said, man, can it sap my days. I always have good intentions to only undertake the task in hand, but so often find myself pulled into something else, or distracted. It's incredibly addictive. We all know that by now.

How many times have you picked up your phone to do something and glanced up at the clock to see you have lost 30 minutes to doomscrolling? Be honest, how many times has glancing at your phone interrupted you reading this book?

I am sure you are fed up with people preaching to you about social media and how we need to cut our overall usage for ourselves, but also importantly, for our teens. That is not what this book is all about. Allowing your teens to have socials or not, is your choice. But do remember just that. It is your choice, not your teens.

During my recent conversations with parents, phones and social media are a common thread. Almost everyone mentioned concerns and worries around the subject, so even though I wanted to skirt around the conversation, I couldn't fully ignore it.

Just like the generations before us, teens, technology and innovation go hand in hand. #Sorrynotsorry.

What seems to have happened with most families I have chatted with, is that devices have been introduced to their children at a fairly young age, to fill boredom and improve behaviour in places like restaurants. Over time this has bled into other moments, with phones becoming a constant in our lives, for most of us.

Many children start out innocently on social media as a form of entertainment, to create dances, play with silly filters and connect with friends.

Worryingly, many of these accounts were signed up for before children reached the age limits set out by social media companies, meaning that if you set your teen up an account when they were 10 and added a fake age of 13 to overcome the age restrictions, by the time they are 13, they are using an account set up to be that of a 16-year-old.

This in turn means that the content they receive is not restricted in the same way as it would be for a child. On some platforms, once certain age limits are hit, teens are then given access to functionalities that are not appropriate for their real ages, such as direct messaging or are being fed adult content and advertising.

Research commissioned by Ofcom in 2022 suggested that almost half (47%) of children aged 8 to 15 with a social media profile have a user age of 16+, while 32% of children aged 8 to 17 have a user age of 18+.

I think it is clear that we should be treating social media with the caution it deserves. Do your research and set boundaries that reflect your family values, just like you do with everything else. There are loads of great books and research out there to support your decision making. Sometimes it is about controlled levels and boundaries, more than instigating a total ban.

Like anything, if you ban it completely people will find a way to get to it anyway.

Look at it this way, you could be bringing your teens up, allowing a small glass of wine or beer during special occasions, but I suspect you wouldn't allow them to have access to an entire liquor cabinet. You certainly wouldn't allow that unsupervised, every day. Every hour even. Think back to the boundaries list you created, what is your stance?

It is becoming very clear to me that social media, and phones as a whole, are having a huge impact on the mental health of our children, on their ability to concentrate and sapping their time like nothing else. I wonder, will we look back on this period of time in years to come, with the same disbelief that we display when recalling children not wearing seatbelts in cars back in the day. (I even travelled home in the boot once).

I do sense a shift overall in people's view of social media, which is positive. There has been more representation in the press discussing the impact social media has on us all, movements created to call for the banning of smartphones for children, led by Australia, seeing governments around the world discussing the part that they need to play in controlling young people's access to social media overall.

I think the most important thing to remember though, is that social media and its addictive nature has not happened by accident. It is not your fault as an individual parent. These platforms have been carefully crafted and continually worked on, in order to make them unputdownable. The tech companies and corporations that have created this problem are culpable. If you are bringing up a teen, right now, they are living alongside social media in a way you have never experienced. It is stitched into their lives more deeply than you can begin to imagine. It's bigger than funny filters and TikTok dances.

Lauren Greenfield's documentary, *Social Society* offers an insightful, balanced view into how social media is dictating the lives of our teens and how hard it is for them to actively choose not to be a part of this world. I highly recommend giving it a watch.

Teens are very easily influenced. Social 'trends' and viral videos have demonstrated that.

Of course, dares have existed as long as children have. Knock and run, prank calls and supplying your substitute teacher with a fake name. For the more extreme among us, only this week I heard of a story told by a 92-year-old, who as a teenager used to find and throw unexploded bombs with his mates. Imagine that going viral.

The internet has supercharged dares, increasing their reach and their impact. Some have been for good, remember the 'ice-bucket challenge' that raised awareness around the disease ALS? Unfortunately as you will know, there is also a more sinister side to trends, such as the 'Blackout Challenge' otherwise known as the choking game, which encouraged young people to choke themselves or hold their breath, in order to film themselves passing out and regaining consciousness. Tragically, it was reported that many children and teens did not survive 'playing' along.

As an adult it is hard to comprehend how you would actively choose to partake in a challenge that has a high risk of injury, let alone try a trend that could leave you dead. Yet, peer pressure has always played a large part in teen life, and social media offers access to a heightened version of that. I am sure we can all remember making a poor decision in the presence of friends or to gain popularity, or just being incredibly curious to try something that you now recognise was a bad idea. That's normal teen behaviour.

All that said, these trends are actually still pretty rare and whilst they are the first 'danger' that pops into many people's heads when discussing social media, in my opinion they don't pose the biggest risk. So what does?

Spend just a few moments on social media and you will notice that you are presented with a feed tailored just for you. The algorithm is created to give you exactly what you want.

If you spend your time searching for recipes, you will be presented with cakes, cooking hacks and air fryer wonders. Lovely.

If you are looking for a holiday, then cue the travel company adverts, beach scenes and top ten cities to visit this year.
*Pass me the credit card.

You've noticed that, haven't you? It's not a coincidence.

If you are looking for ways to lose weight, watch porn or are struggling with your mental health, guess what you are going to get? An abundance of unhealthy content sent straight to the palm of your hand. The more curious you become, the deeper you will travel. The phenomenon of negative bias means these generous tech companies will ensure you are fed more troubling content than uplifting. We will discuss that in more detail shortly.

Pair that with carefully curated content from influencers, filters, AI and unrealistic beauty and lifestyle standards and you are in a world so far from your own, it is easy to start to feel more than a little lost. Especially at a vulnerable age.

Realistically, if you don't have limits placed on your phone, there is no getting away or hiding from these influences. It needn't be anything as extreme as partaking in a viral trend, just the constant pressure of external influence and the voices of peers that are ever present. They reach you in your bedroom, your lounge, at the dinner table and even in the toilet. There is no escaping it.

Ofcom states that two thirds of teens and young adults have recently encountered at least one potentially harmful piece of content online, but only around one in six go on to report it.

I don't want to sound melodramatic but whilst it can be a fun source of entertainment, social media has the ability to destroy not just our teens, but our society, if it is left to freewheel.

Our sense of self builds during early teen years in particular, naturally the people we surround ourselves with help to shape who we become. So consider then, if the main influence during teen years becomes social media, which prioritises a fabricated and polished version of others, how do we see the truth?

How can we expect our teens to become an authentic version of themselves?

How can they build healthy levels of self-esteem when they are always comparing themselves to unrealistic standards?

How can they know the truth about anything, when their main source of information is not verified, or gleaned from peers who lack experience.

By allowing our teens' main form of influence to become the strangers they interact with online, are we allowing these people to shape them? That's our job, not theirs.

Stay curious

Your job is not done yet.

Stay curious about your teens life.
Keep a view on who they are friends with, what they do in their free time and who they are interacting with online.

"I don't understand", is never a valid excuse to not be present. If you don't understand their world or their tech then learn. Ask questions, teach yourself.

Taking it back

It is hard to take away something you have already gifted.

Social media is a prime example of this.

> **"If they haven't got it they feel like an outsider. If I don't let them have it, I feel like an outsider."**
>
> **AROUND THE TABLE**

If your teen has never had an account on a social media platform before, then it is probably an easier call now, than it was a few years back, to say no to signing up in the first place. Collectively it seems more parents are saying no to joining social media until their teens are older. There is comfort in that, as no one (even us adults) wants to be the odd one out, or cause their teen to be left out.

If you are considering revoking social media, then try and approach it with compassion. It is understandable that your teen will be unhappy, angry and will likely try and find a way around it.

Prep the idea in advance, explain your reasoning and share some of the evidence that is coming to light surrounding the damage that social media can do. There are initiatives set up by parents and teachers now too, that encourage parents to form a collective, so that no one teen feels alone in this decision. That could make it easier.

But let's not kid ourselves. If your teen already has an account and you choose to revoke it, it will not be easy. However, given that it could improve their wellbeing, their focus and their happiness, would it be worth the initial pain? If they were addicted to anything else you would make those steps.

Get comfortable in feeling uncomfortable.

Make the decision you know you have to. Tell it as it is. Stop tiptoeing around the important stuff. Your job is to keep your teen safe and rounded, not perpetually happy.

If you decide to allow them to keep social media here are a few recommendations:

- Set clear boundaries around device usage and social media.

- Insist on full access to their device/phone. You are not saying you need to pry or check it every day, but you should have the password and be able to perform spotchecks.

- Keep on top of current trends.

- Don't be an ostrich; no good comes out of keeping your head in the sand. It's your job to dig and understand what is going on with your teen when it comes to their online footprint.

- Be aware that teens, as we did, will find a way around even the strictest of limits if they want to. There are even browsers out there, just like Google, that are completely private and are able to avoid parental controls along with social and porn apps that are designed to look like mundane icons, such as calculators. It is important to stay on top of this technology and carry out regular phone monitoring.

Don't forget, it is your responsibility as a parent to keep them safe, not to keep them happy.

> "Phones made parenting teens really tough. With my daughter there was a lot of bullying, they were trying to control her and make her feel excluded. Girls were ganging up and saying really horrible things, I was finding nasty texts that people had written about her. It was a really challenging time. It was really, really hard navigating that. I felt really isolated, you just want to make everything go away, you want them to feel good about themselves and just seeing them losing confidence is hard. It's hard trying to build up their self-esteem and self-worth."
>
> **AROUND THE TABLE**

One for sorrow, two for joy

It was a good day. I had managed the school run with no drama, managed to squeeze in a quick swim at our local pool and was heading back home to write. Walking over to my car I spotted a magpie. Now, I am not particularly superstitious, but 'one for sorrow' always enters my head whenever I see a solo magpie. I caught myself thinking, 'well there goes my good day'.

But then I considered how ridiculous it was to allow your perception of your whole day, to be changed by one thought. I waited and watched the magpie skip across the car park, to his mate, who I hadn't noticed until I slowed up. Ahh, 'two for joy'.

I wonder how many times we see a single magpie, assume that it is solo and therefore adopt negativity, when in fact there could be another just over the way if we only took the time to look for it.

Negative bias is not a new revelation. It has been long studied and is a vital part of our psychology. In basic terms, it is widely thought that humans prefer to pay attention to things that are negative, more than they do those things that are positive. Soroka, Fournier and Nir (2019) studied peoples reactions to video news content across 17 countries, with their results indicating that humans are indeed, more aroused and generally attentive to negative news above positive.

Imagine you were walking down a street on your way to meet a friend. On the way you see a really cute dog, like the cutest. It was maybe even carrying a little teddy in its mouth. See I told you, the cutest. You smile and continue, but then you see another dog. It snarls and snaps at you on the way past, bearing its teeth. It's really aggressive. Scary stuff.

What don't your parents understand about you?
❝ Sometimes I just want to be left alone.

The chances are, when you reach your friend you will be more likely to tell them about the aggressive dog than the cute one, because the negative experience is given more weight in your mind. Thanks brain.

Johann Hari states in his book *Stolen Focus* that this knowledge was adopted by the big tech firms, and used to influence the design of the algorithms within social media. Whilst some of the evidence to support this theory is still pretty new, it is clear that when you scroll on social media, every movement is monitored. This data is valuable to advertisers and tech companies alike. How long you linger, the pace at which you move on and which posts you interact with, all paint a picture of what you like and what you don't. Kerching, this is a big money business. It means you can be categorised by your interests and successfully sold to by companies that match your tastes.

Taking negativity bias into consideration, it is to be expected that as a mere human being, you will linger for longer on negative content. It's quite literally a morbid fascination. The thing is, the more you linger on the negative, the more the algorithm presents you with similar content. So, ultimately we are left stuck in a loop. The algorithm gives us more of what we 'want', and as a result, that's often filled with negativity.

Johann uses this example:

"Picture two teenage girls who go to the same party, and then go home on the same bus. One of them posts a video that says they had a great time and loved it. The other posts an angry rant calling all the girls at the party skanks and all the boys pricks. The algorithms scan the kind of language you use—and they'll put the first video into a few people's feeds, and the second video into far more people's feeds—because angry and hostile content makes people 'engage'. You'll post back: what do you mean they were skanks? You're the skank. And on it goes.

This is bad enough at the level of two teenage girls (and we all know what's happened to teenage mental health). But now imagine a whole country where the kindest, sanest voices—arguing for moderation, decency, compromise—are muffled and pushed back, and the cruelest, most toxic voices are pushed to the front. Except you don't have to imagine that. We've been living it for years now – with all the catastrophic effects on our political and collective attention."

So is there a very real risk, that the content we are all absorbing will become perpetually negative? On top of that, life is unpredictable. You don't always have a choice over what is thrown your way. You do, however, have a responsibility to your teen to support them through the ups and downs of life, to keep turning up, no matter how bad or frustrating it gets. You can teach them how to deal with negativity, about negative bias and to remember that no matter what, you do always have a choice in how you deal with a situation. Positivity, on the whole, is a choice. There is always a little light to be found, even in the most difficult of moments, even if it is just a lesson to be had. Try to find it, and encourage your teen to do the same by voicing moments when you are finding things tough, but are able to see the positivity that will follow.

Say it louder and prouder.

Give yourself credit when it is due. You may be the only person your teen ever hears saying "I am proud of myself" out loud.

"Only boring people get bored."

I had a teacher that used to say 'Only boring people get bored'.
It used to frustrate me as I was bored, an awful lot of the time.
Not because I was 'boring', but because I was often left to my
own devices, both during the week whilst my mum worked, or at
weekends when my dad would be out in the garden.

I think the message was meant to be, if you are bored find something
to do. If you are a creative person this will come easily. And I
guess, for the most part it did. Back in the 90's, long before the term
doomscroll even existed I would always be able to keep myself
busy. I would create crafts projects, snuggle up and read and reread
Matilda, watch a VHS movie on repeat and set up practical jokes and
'traps' for my dad's current girlfriend. Sadly, it turns out that pepper
floats if you put it in tea, I should have stuck to the salt.

But, if you just get bored and sit within that, is that so bad? Wow, I
would love the opportunity to be bored now, wouldn't you? My brain
is a constant conveyor belt of things I have to action, jobs I need to
complete, places everyone else needs to be. Maybe that is a notion
that has changed since smartphones and computers have arrived.
Maybe now, only the least boring people get bored?

I asked both my son and daughter when they were last bored. Both
replied, at school, during lessons they didn't enjoy.

I questioned whether that is in fact boredom or simply unrest at
doing something or being somewhere you don't want to be? When I

reminisced about being bored when I was young, it was different. It was those moments when you felt uncomfortable in your own skin, because you had absolutely nothing to do. Nothing. To. Do.

I recall what felt like hours, waiting for my mum to finish a cleaning job. I sat in a stranger's spare room with little more to do than spot patterns in the woodchip, because *Power Rangers* had finished and now it was time for the lunchtime news. Yawn. By week 3, it led me to scouring the bookcases and reading *Little Dorrit* by Charles Dickens at the age of nine.

> **"I really think everyone should do some sort of hobby, club or activity that they enjoy. Even if it's a park run on a Saturday morning, it's free and fun. I just think being part of a community or being part of something or other is so, so beneficial."**
>
> **AROUND THE TABLE**

We are living in a world of constants, where many of us are never given the grace of experiencing boredom, owing to busy lives combined with excessive phone usage. Even our intake of general entertainment has become one long flow of information, continual scrolling, the news is being fed to us 24/7, even if there is nothing of merit to report. Busy, busy, busy.

I try to enhance opportunities for boredom in my children as often as possible, mostly by heavily restricting screen time. I don't get it right all the time. When I am busy or distracted, I often lose my focus or let extra device time slip, but I try to keep on top of it. When screen time is limited, not just for teens but us adults too, I witness a lightness. It gives everyone more time and more space. Turns out we are nicer, more creative and happier when we are bored.

Curiosity thrives with boredom

Not sure where to start?

It is tricky to know how much time to allow phones for, I can't answer that. It's your choice.
For us, we never allow phones before 8am. Having sunshine before social media, sets you up for a better and brighter day.

To give some element of choice, I allow our teens to pick times they would like to be able to use their phone, within an 11 hour window. So 8am-7pm or 9am-8pm. Then, on top of that, I used to go super stingy and limit overall usage for each day, to an amount that I see fit. It was usually an hour, but during school holidays, this would be more if they want to talk to friends or are out and about more and need to contact me or others. I monitor their phones still, but nowadays they tend to keep their usage to a low level themselves, without the need for me to add time restrictions.

Dear teen,

Step into your truth.

A true version of yourself is the most powerful thing you can become.

The vase

What is mine can never be yours and what is yours can never be mine.

That is the interesting thing about perspective. The unwavering ownership of it. A collection of people can seemingly all be experiencing exactly the same thing, at exactly the same time but it will never be anyone else's experience, other than yours.

Like when you hand a friend a book that you have loved, or play them a song, but they don't like it like you do. It feels disappointing, like they have taken the shine away, but they can't help it. Even if they profess to like it as much as you, they cannot like it in the same way, it will not connect with them for exactly the same reasons. Because they are not you. You can never truly understand how it makes them feel, even if they tell you.

Aside from their genetic makeup, millions of moments inform the person that they are and how they behave and feel, at any one time. These moments are both significant and insignificant. Notable and simply not. Even those brought up together, by the same parents, do not share the same perspective.

The way in which you have brought your children up will likely bring their perspective closer to yours than that of others, but it will never match. That's worth remembering when imploring your teen to see your point of view.

Dear teen,

Imagine you and your parent(s) are all sitting around a table, there is a vase in the centre filled with flowers.

You can all recognise that the jug is there. You all see it has flowers in it. You can all agree on that. From your position around the table though, you can never see the other side of the vase, unless you sit where your parents are sitting. They may be able to see a flower that you cannot. You may be able to spot a colour reflecting on the porcelain, due to the light coming through a window on your side.

However hard they try, they can not fully see the vase, or the flowers from where you are, unless they take your seat.

Try and remember that, sometimes, when you are assuming your parents do not understand, it is actually that they are just not sitting in your seat, and you too are choosing not to sit in theirs.

The notebook

My daughter left her notebook open up on the kitchen table.
I wrote a little note in it to tell her that I love her, decorated it with hearts and placed it on her bed.

When I went to bed that night the notebook laid open on my pillow, with a note returned to me.

I wrote back and our penpalship continued for a few days, back and forth. With each asking the other questions. Old school texting I guess, but it felt I could ask her anything as she would write back honestly.

I hope, whenever she sees the notepad waiting for her, she feels the same whisper of joy that I do whenever I see it waiting, open for me.

Generational trauma

I saw a video on social media the other day, demonstrating how trauma is passed through generations, using 4 glasses filled with water.

The water in the first glass was dark and murky, representing a grandparents personal trauma. This was tipped into the next glass, which was already full of clean water. Of course the two merge, but the murky water is diluted. With each tip into the next glass, or generation, the water clears a little. Therapy, in this video, was represented by a large jug of fresh water being tipped into the final glass, until it overflowed, causing the dark residue of the initial water to disappear completely.

In an ideal world, we would all receive therapy before becoming parents. There are few, if any, of us that have brought up a child in this world and managed to do so without imparting our own fears, experiences or trauma on them in some way. We are human, it is natural to want to protect our children from that which has hurt us.

But your fears do not have to be theirs. Or yours, for that matter.

We are born with only two fears, a fear of falling and a fear of loud noises. Everything else is a learned behaviour. I was told a story of a lady who formed a phobia of buttons. It seems impossible for most to be scared of something so seemingly benign. In actual fact this lady had been a child when the phobia formed, her mother had been buttoning her coat to leave a party at the very same time a balloon loudly popped behind her. Her brain raced to a conclusion that the buttons were the cause. This thought was verified and then cemented by her parent also jumping and then rushing her away from the party without comfort or explanation. It was clear, buttons were the problem.

At 13

" Girls can be superheroes too.

Regulate

I am sitting in the garden room that belongs to my therapist Kirsty. It's peaceful here, and that is not an accident. Kirsty has crafted a space that fosters peace, away from the chaos of the world.

In an interesting twist, it's been me asking her the questions today. Given her experience, the one I am particularly hooked on is "If you could only give one piece of advice to parents of teens, what would it be?"

And, lucky for you I am not in the market of gatekeeping. There is no need to leave a comment stating TEEN below or to sign up for an intensive course. I am going to give you the information simply based on the agreement that you will listen and action the advice that Kirsty has gifted to us all.

"I would say to teach your teen how to regulate their emotions and teach yourself how to do the same."

I am sure you are familiar with the term 'regulate emotions', but do you really understand what it means and how you can factor it into your parenting. It can be hard to confront our emotions head on but emotional regulation encourages you to do just that. It needn't be scary though, the more you practise the more natural it becomes.

In simple terms, 'regulating emotions' refers to consciously taking the time to understand, process and manage the way you are feeling.

It can help you to adaptively cope with different situations, and helps to prevent kneejerk reactions and impulsive behaviours. In my personal experience it also helps to eliminate feelings of guilt and shame.

As with many of the techniques we have discussed, make no mistake, this chapter is just as important for you to take on board, as it is for your teen. It's longer than most of the previous sections too. Stick with me, it will be worth the read.

Regulating your emotions will enable you to be less reactive, less stressed and to prioritise what actually matters. These are all really valuable tools to have at any stage of life, but never more so than when you are supporting a teen, who also has a need to access all of the above. It is natural if your teen is sad, angry or frustrated to want to fix it, by making them happy. But distractions can only last for so long. We can't fix everything on behalf of our teens, and even if we could we shouldn't. We should instead be providing them with the tools to help themselves.

Regulating emotions allows you space to notice how situations, people and even your own thoughts, make you feel. It prevents you from withholding or burying feelings such as anger or fear. It stops you feeling like your emotions are controlling you and rather lets the emotions run through you.

It is all too easy to feel an emotion and react to it impulsively. If you feel anger, you may lash out. If you are feeling insecure, you may be more likely to give into peer pressure and make bad choices.

Right, that all sounds great on paper doesn't it, but how do we access this skill? Together with Kirsty, these simple and actionable steps have been crafted to help you to connect with, and regulate your emotions when you are feeling overwhelmed.

1 Make space

When it comes to learning how to regulate emotions, the most important thing is to allow yourself the time and the space to do so. You need to forge a moment without any distractions, whether it's your phone, TV, other people or something else, put it all to one side. It's really important that everybody has that downtime where they just stop. Find a space that grants you silence.

2 Breathe

Take some nice soothing breaths, just tune in and use this control over your breath, to just slow everything down.

3 Sit with it

Ask yourself, "What do I feel right now?".
Take a moment to sit in the feeling. Just sit with it. There's no need to fear it. It's all part of life. Even though this emotion feels really uncomfortable right now. Acknowledge; "I'm just going to sit with this for a moment and use my breath to gently work through it". When you use your breath in this way, it allows your nervous system to calm down, then you can see everything more clearly. It's almost like you're taking a step out of the thoughts and the feelings to allow you to review them from a distance.

4 Get curious

Start to look at what is just underneath the emotion you are feeling. Consider "Why did I react this way?". Don't allow yourself to cast judgement on yourself or the situation, approach the question in a really gentle and curious way. Ask "Why did I get so upset/angry/sad". Often if you get angry it's because underneath it all, you feel scared or hurt or anxious. Take the time to recognise what made you feel the way you are feeling.

5 Recognise patterns

If you have had an incident or an emotional reaction to something that has happened, it is also important to ask yourself

"Why did I react that way to what happened?". Consider what could have triggered your response. For example, it might be that there are certain smells, places or situations that make you feel anxious/happy/stressed. It might be that a particular person makes you feel a certain way. Sometimes our emotions can be a result of being reminded of a past experience. Ask yourself, 'What does this remind me of?' It could be that a perfume or aftershave triggers a memory for example, and causes a powerful emotional response.

The most important part is not to run from these feelings, just sit within them and feel what you are feeling.

4 What now?
Consider what you need to do to feel better. Can you accept the emotion and move on or do you need to work through it further? Maybe there are external factors at play such as a lack of sleep? Are you feeling burnt out?

At this stage it is important to consider what you need in order to resolve what you are feeling right now. Is there anything that you need more of? Is there anything that you need less of? Is there anything that's on your mind that you really need to speak to somebody about and share?

5 Do something creative
Taking the time to be creative can be a really useful way to access how you are feeling and sit with it, if just focusing on the feeling alone feels too much. Find something you love that allows you to connect with your emotions: drawing, journalling, songwriting, dancing, poetry. The choice is yours.

What can you do to help your teen?
If they're feeling stressed or burnt out your teen is likely to feel more emotional. Make sure that they are getting enough exercise, they're eating properly, they're getting enough relaxation and good night's

sleep (well as much as you can), just try to recognise what triggers them to feel more emotional.

A daily check-in is a great call, just ask "How are you feeling today?"

Lead by example

It was a week that I felt really, really stressed out. Things had not gone my way. I had experienced some disappointment at work and a 2 day migraine had meant a deadline was slipping away from me. Rather than keeping it from my teens I gave them a quick synopsis of how I was feeling, then I went on to explain what emotion it made me feel and what I did to make myself feel better.

"I had a tough day today, I had a migraine which made me feel frustrated because it slowed me up and ruined my plans. I guess it left me feeling angry. I couldn't stay with that emotion all day so I went for a swim, as that helps to clear my head. I feel much better now."

Showing your teens that you're experiencing similar things to them, bridges the gap between you. Show them that it is normal to feel emotions, that you won't feel happy all the time.

I will leave you with this little summary from Kirsty.

"It's really important to know what helps to make you feel better and to ask for help. It is absolutely normal to feel these emotions, to sit with them and to know that they will always pass. You will have to do that without distraction with no phones or anything else, you know, just sit with it, breathe, journal, write it down.

And yeah, and then move on to all the nice self-care stuff. Find things that make you feel good. But just learning how to talk about it is really important for parents and children alike."

Dear teen,

When the world seems heavy, overwhelming or when things feel like they are running away with you, take a breath. These techniques may help you find your way:

1. Talk to an adult you trust about how you are feeling. A parent is a great place to start (but we would say that right). If you think you would benefit from extra support, ask for a daily check in with someone. Just a minute each day, to talk to them about how you are feeling.

2. Practice gratitude - this doesn't need to be some whacky woo-woo approach to your wellbeing, it's just straight talking about what is good in your life. Say three things out loud, daily, that you are thankful to have in your life and why. For example, it could be your dog, because they always welcome you when you get in from school.

3. Pray (or just talk out loud) - whether you are religious or not, 'praying' to something or someone bigger than the moment you are in, gives us a sense of who we are. Pick your style, it could be a God, a lost relative, mother nature or the universe. Whoever or whatever you choose, talk to them out loud. Treat them like a friend; ask them for direction, tell them how you are feeling, ask for a favour or be curious. Yes I know it can feel unnatural to start with, but just get talking.

4. Exercise. You don't need to be breaking records, just move your body daily. As an individual having a workout, playing a team sport or just dancing in your bedroom. Just move.

5. Don't box up or run from the feeling. It is ok to not always feel ok.

Dogs

> **ff** Do not be in a hurry to 'fix' **JJ**
> things. Rather, enrich your
> understanding in the evergoing
> process of discovery and
> finding more the cause of your
> ignorance.
> - Bruce Lee

Imagine you are sitting in a room. You are using the only chair.

It's large enough to feel comfortable in the space, but small enough to have considered it.

The door opens and a dog walks in.

This dog represents an emotion.

You are not the emotion that you feel, in the same way you are not the dog, but still this dog comes into the room and sits with you.

You have a choice, you can sit with the dog, or you can leave. Either way the dog will remain in the room. Doing its thing.

This dog is a happy little thing. Chances are you'll want to hang around, he is fluffy, fun and playful. He makes you happy. In fact, he is happiness.
The door opens again and in struts a big, aggressive looking dog. I mean, he is really mad.

He spots happiness and chases him right out of the door. Snarling. Snapping. That makes you angry. You were having a good time with happiness. This dude though, he's anger.

Now you have a choice. You can up and leave, or you can stay with anger.

The thing is, if you leave, anger is still going to be here. Undealt with.

You try instead to calm him. It doesn't work straight away. You watch him for a while, from a distance. Then you spot something. A thorn in his side.

Cautiously you approach. It's not easy but you manage to quickly and gently remove the thorn. He calms.

You pass him some food, throw a ball maybe. He is like a different dog.

Before long he begins to trust you. You decide to do something risky, You open the door and invite happiness back in, slowly.

Something happens. Instead of charging this time anger is calmer. He acknowledges happiness, but does not attack. He relaxes. He isn't too interested when happiness approaches you, and curls up on your lap. Before long, anger leaves.

You have a choice, to sit with your emotions. It is important that you do. This allows you to pay attention to what they are telling you. Listen to the message. But understand you are not them. You are never the dog.

Dear teen,

You are not the emotions you are feeling.

They are a signal to ignite your curiosity. Let it be.
Don't rush to answer their call.
Sit with it. Take your time.
Question it deeply before you react.
What is this emotion actually trying to tell you?

Sometimes fear presents itself as anger.
Sometimes loneliness presents itself as jealousy.

By really paying attention to the emotions you are feeling, you will be able to work out what you need to do, in order to feel better.

Remember, that may just mean talking through your feelings with someone. Always ask for help if you need it.

Learn who needs what, when.

Have you found the sweet spot yet to connect with your teen? When are they most open to you?

The car, just before bed, first thing over breakfast? Pay attention to the patterns. What works and what doesn't.

In our house my daughter wants to sit and chat first thing, or straight after school and prefers her own time to chill before bed, whereas talking to my son after school has always been like getting blood from a stone, but he is connected and animated late in the evening.

NB. It has not passed me by that they have also found my patterns over the years, speak to mum before bed and it delays lights off, right?

At 13 " Be careful who you let into your inner circle.

Grace

This chapter is dedicated to Grace.

I was introduced to Ruth, Grace's mum, through a mutual friend. Ruth spends much of her time supporting others who find themselves in a similar situation to that of Ruth and her own daughter, during her teenage years. .

As soon as I learnt of their story, I knew that it was impossible to write this book without Grace becoming a part of it. When I tentatively reached out to Ruth, she assured me that she loves talking about Grace. So, one November afternoon, that is exactly what we did.

This single chapter is of course, not the full story of Grace as a person. I could never do that justice. I could never fully understand the power of her character, the moments only her family shared, the in betweens, the laughter and the love.

What I tell is just one part of her journey. Sadly one that ended far before it should. Grace died by suicide in 2018 just before her 19th birthday.

I hope by reading about Grace, it will heighten your awareness and help you to recognise if you, or someone around you needs help. Please reach out to a professional or your support network if that is the case.

As a little one, Grace was her family's warrior princess. Sweet, kind and unassuming.

Primary school wasn't always easy for Grace, so when it came to progressing to senior school, Ruth hoped it would give her a fresh start, for a couple of years this worked out well. Grace made a new, small group of friends and seemed happy. After a while though, the dynamic changed when a new member joined the group and Grace was increasingly pushed out. She was made to feel like she didn't belong and told that she was annoying.

"At the time, I didn't join the dots. At every parent's evening her work was fine, she was an average student, but the teachers would all say "We'd love to hear more from Grace in class. She's really quiet." I knew she was generally quiet in social situations, but at home she wasn't particularly, certainly not in a way that I would worry. In the safety of home, she was still very often the little 'warrior child' that I knew. When she started to experience trouble with some girls within her friend group at school, I just thought, "Oh, she's a teenager, she needs to be working these friendships out for herself."

I deliberately chose to not get too involved. Of course I would suggest "Why don't you do this" or "Have you thought about this". Looking back she was actually in and out of the school nurse quite a lot with stomach aches, I would get a phone call to say Grace isn't feeling well quite regularly, so that did make me start to worry. I tried talking with her a few times about how she was feeling, but she would tell me "I just don't like school". She would say "I just don't always feel like I'm fitting. I like being at home more. I'm fine when I'm at home. Don't worry about it".

I feel a bit of regret for that time, but I don't think it was ever that she didn't feel she could tell me about it. I have wondered if she had the thought in the back of her head, if I tell mum the whole story, she's going to come in all guns blazing to try and fix it, and that will make it 10 times worse. Maybe that would have been the case."

It turned out that Grace was being pushed out of her friendship group, and bullied.

After the upset for Grace continued, Ruth did go on to speak to the school about the problems she was facing, but things were not really taken seriously enough.

"I did eventually go in and speak with the school and they were very unhelpful at the time. I didn't call it bullying, as I just thought it was some girls being unkind. The school didn't call it bullying either, but when I look back now, it is clear to me that it was and should have been treated as such. These girls were continually being unkind to Grace for no good reason and it was a targeted campaign against her alone, which lasted at least a couple of years. It bothers me that Grace never got validation for the fact that she was bullied, all the way through to when she died."

After Grace died, Ruth read her journals and watched videos that Grace had created of herself talking; they painted an extensive picture of Grace's thoughts and feelings at the time.

"They've decided I'm annoying, so if I don't say anything, I can't say anything annoying."

Grace had made a vow of silence with herself. This silence grew into anxiety over time which started to affect other areas of her life for a while. She became quieter and found social settings harder to navigate.

"The anxiety kind of got worse and worse. When she was around 16 I remember trying to encourage her to be a bit braver, just pretending I needed something from the shop and I couldn't park. I'd say "Grace, can you just hop out and grab some chewing gum" but she would sit in the car just going "I can't, I can't". It was like she was too afraid to be in her own skin to just pop into a shop. That's when I suppose I started thinking, this anxiety is a real problem. If you're afraid to go into a shop where you don't even need to speak, or if you're afraid to open the front door when it's just the postman, it's at the stage where it is affecting your life heavily.

I tried to have numerous conversations with her about it, giving her tips on how to be in groups and how to have conversations. I would say, "You don't have to talk about yourself if you don't want to, you know, you just ask someone a question or pay them a compliment", but she wasn't able to take that on board very easily. It was hard for her."

When Grace left school things started to get a bit better, away from that group of girls she seemed to relax into her own skin and she went to college. She found two good friends and even secured a place at Winchester University. "She was really looking forward to that."

Soon after, Grace started an internship, which involved doing office tasks such as answering the phone and welcoming clients. At this point Grace's anxiety and depression worsened. Grace journaled and made videos of herself during this time, often chastising herself and her behaviour.

"She would continually be imploring herself to be braver, to be more. She didn't need to be."

The videos Grace had created around this time indicated how these simple tasks really worried her on a daily basis. She put a huge amount of pressure on herself about getting everything perfect at work, and her anxiety and depression worsened.

"I can't tell them, because they'll just think I'm useless and a waste of space. I have to do it. I have to do it."

Ruth told me that if the pandemic of 2020 had come sooner, she believes it would have saved her. "The world needed to stop for a while so she could just focus on herself and get better. When I talk now, with young people about their depression and suicidal thoughts, I tend to explain to them that the depression they feel should be treated as a 'thought cancer'. When people are diagnosed with a high grade of cancer, everything else has to stop, so that the cancer can be treated, dealt with and hopefully managed. When we are diagnosed with depression we are expected to carry on as normal, but we just can't."

And maybe she is right, we often use distraction and positivity to patch over how we are really feeling, we try to work towards the next thing. We do it as parents too, trying to override negative feelings with those of optimism. That could be getting a new group of friends, finishing school, going to university, anything that seems positive and in the future. But we often ignore the real problem and depression isn't something that just goes away by ignoring it. Suicidal thoughts are not something we just get over by doing something happy. We need professional support.

At the end of 2017, Grace faced an acute mental health crisis, spiralling into a dark depression. In March 2018 Grace could no longer see a way out. She took her own life, two weeks before her 19th birthday.

It is clear throughout this conversation that hindsight is a cruel thing. Ruth tries not to rerun the past in order to walk a path to a different outcome, because of course, there sadly cannot be one for Grace or her family.

There is little benefit in dwelling on the 'what might have beens', and yet as I listen to Ruth talk about the incredible work she now does, working alongside others suffering in similar ways to Grace, I question how she is able. How can she hold it together? How will her wounds ever have a chance to heal, when she is revisiting these thoughts every day. But then, when someone loses a child, I doubt that the wounds will ever heal fully. By revisiting thoughts of Grace continually, her memory and legacy only grows.

I ask, "If you had the opportunity to do so, would you go back and read Grace's journals while she was alive?" "No" Ruth tells me with certainty "That would be a step too far, it would be an invasion of her privacy".

It strikes me that this is yet another line we constantly walk as parents, between privacy and safety. Between right and wrong. Between what we believe is right and what we want. Honestly I do not know what I would do. Checking my teens phone is one thing, given that they are fully aware that I do so. But their journals? They need something that is sacred, don't they? Something that belongs to them alone. We all need that.

I asked Ruth if there is anything she would like to pass to you, the reader. She gave me this fantastic technique to share, which I found really visual and supportive and have used since with my own family. Here's hoping you will find it helpful too:

Dear teen,

Imagine you are carrying a pot around, it is where you carry all your worries, woes, thoughts, feelings and secrets. Any thoughts that are stuck with you, that you are unsure about and are not dealing with fully, will build up in the pot.

After a while you will notice the pot gets heavy. Sometimes too heavy to handle and carry around.

You will notice that the pot has a valve at the bottom. When it is opened, it lets some of those feelings run out in a controlled way. If you don't open the valve often enough, sometimes the pot can start overflowing and you can feel out of control.

It is important to know, you have options to keep your pot at a manageable state.

1. The valve can be opened by doing things that feel good, make you happier, joyful or give you pleasure. It is affected too by your brain hormones, so it can also be released by doing things like exercise, tasks that take some work before you are rewarded such as making your bed or other household jobs.

2. Your parents or the trusted adults around you, have bigger pots than you, meaning there is always space for some of your thoughts to be stored in theirs, until you have the space to deal with them. You just need to tell them what it is you would like them to hold. They don't need to offer an opinion, they can just listen if that is best for you.

Think about it as if you were to go on holiday, you wouldn't pack everyone's stuff all in one big bag and expect it to be carried by one person, so why should you carry everything you are feeling yourself.

3. At any time you can take some of the weight out of your pot, and pass it to a parent to hold on to. You needn't tell them what it is. Just physically hold the thought in your hand and ask that they keep it for while. They can then pop it in a jewellery case or a box, tucked away for as long as you need a break from it. If it helps you work through the thought or feeling you could pop it in a ring box in your pocket for a day and see if it makes it easier to deal with. Carrying it around separately for a while can offer a unique perspective.

If you are having trouble with a certain thought or feeling that is too hard to handle, speak to someone straight away. If you are feeling overwhelmed, scared or like you have nowhere to go, know that there is always someone out there to help and support you. You just need to ask.

Whilst writing about Grace, I was reminded of a farewell speech performed by Joe Tracini, performed at the Norwich Theatre Royal a few years back. It has stuck with me ever since:

"When I first started telling tales, I realised that people only really told stories at bedtime, but I think that's a waste. You should tell stories in the morning in case you need a bit of help getting up. A long time ago I didn't feel like I was enough, some people told me that I didn't belong at home and that made me feel worse. Some days I didn't even get out of bed, it was like getting up with some sort of curse. But I was comparing me to the rest of the world and that's massive. It doesn't matter how much good I give, I'm always going to be smaller than earth. Look, I'm going to tell you all a secret, but once I've told you, that is that, you'll never see life the same again and you can never get life back.

All our hearts are good and bad, and they keep fighting every day.
The beat we feel inside, one wins, one goes away.
We hope that it's the good that wins, but sometimes it's the bad.
But either way, each day starts again, and another go is had.
When waking up doesn't feel worth it, somebody somewhere always cares.

We can all add good to someone's world just by being there.
All the things that make life special, all the colours, sounds and tastes.
They'd all lose the touch of magic if your goodness went to waste.
Hope is more than wishful thinking but it's less than certain sight.
Hope is knowing behind darkness life is always hiding light.
Hope is never a decision; you don't choose the hope you lose.
But if you're here you're never hopeless because hope beats the hearts we use.

All that anybody wants is to be seen and loved and heard.

Before you go, I hope you know, true love is something you deserve.
So, goodnight until tomorrow, and never forget what I have said.
That someone's world always gets brighter, because you get out of bed."

It's not all about you

Teens don't make decisions just to spite you. In fact most of the time they don't spare you a thought. It's not an act of deception or defiance, just a bad choice in the moment.

At
13
" All the things that scare you won't come to pass.

Plasticine

I find it fascinating watching how teens are formed and moulded so easily by who and what they are surrounded by the most. Maybe we all are.

Eating up quotes, opinions and fallacies and regurgitating them as facts. Changing their mind like the wind, chasing trends and causes.

Your teen will not always have the same opinion as you. It would actually be a bit weird if they did, but there is a beauty in that.

Do you remember being a teen and discovering new things, that felt like they were just your own, like you were the first person in the world that had found it. Even better, that feeling of connecting with someone else your own age over something you both felt super passionately about.

I envy that ability to feel so deeply connected with something. Be it a cause, a statement or a crush. As an adult I don't seem to be able to access that level of passion so freely nowadays.

That's one of the things I love about having teens, that they challenge my opinions and versions of events with new and fresh ideas. They keep me curious and bring conversations to the room that would otherwise be passing me by. They help me to grow too, by calling me out if I am holding on to old-fashioned views and I am not sure if you can empathise, but they certainly don't hold back on the piss-taking either.

In a similar vein, I have always found there is strength in upholding multi-generational friendships, they tend to shine a light from a different direction, giving us insight and knowledge that we could not otherwise access from our standpoint alone. Bringing up teens is just as rewarding, if only you take the time to listen to what they have to say.

> **❝ Show me your friends and I will ❞ show you your future**
> **- Dan Pena**

But what happens if the opinion is considered extreme or worrying on some level, if it is fueled by hate or discrimination? Due to their malleable nature, you may find yourself calling their opinions into question from time to time. This is often amplified from external influences, sadly, you don't need to look far to find hate speech, misogyny, discrimination and misinformation, all freely available for our teens to absorb. It is pumped through all of our social feeds and seeps into classrooms and conversations, twisting their narratives. The worst part is this unrest is growing, due to, you've got it, negative bias and algorithms.

A study from the University of Kent in 2024* indicated that TikTok was actively amplifying misogynistic content to young people. During a study of over 1000 videos on TikTok, it was found that the recommender systems (powered by algorithms) actively amplify and direct harmful content to young people. *Their research paper 'Safer scrolling: How algorithms popularise and gamify online hate and misogyny for young people' is published by the Association of School and College Leaders.

After just 5 days, researchers saw a FOURFOLD increase in the level of misogynistic content shown on an individual's TikTok account.

They discovered that TikTok privileges more extreme material and through increased usage, users are exposed to more and more misogynistic ideologies.

So in basic terms, the more you view, the more is presented to you.

The content is gamified through soft or humorous cultural forms, which I assume helps to make it more appealing to young people. Fun hey!

This is a problem for all of our children, whether or not your teen is using social media. These messages are being filtered into society as "normal behaviour", often masked with humour.

Due to the combined exposure of online and offline information, it can be really hard for young people to navigate what is true and what is not.

I guess in part that is why social media can be so damaging. Beyond the conversations of their friend groups, these sometimes questionable values are also continually reaffirmed by strangers and the media, able to reach them wherever they are via that little device in their hand.

Now I am all for debating new trends and stances, but when it comes to parenting there is a clear difference between a differing opinion, and your teen forming a belief that is fundamentally damaging for them and society as a whole.

So how is best to handle those moments, if your teen forms and broadcasts an opinion that is potentially dangerous?

It is a natural instinct to just shut it down as quickly as possible. Tell them they are wrong and put a rule in place to prevent the subject being spoken about again. That approach can do more harm than good.

Let's use misogyny as an example.

There are currently many high profile figures, actively supporting misogynistic viewpoints online. Your teen may have already encountered posts, particularly if you are raising boys, that sell the benefits of growing masculine power by degrading and/or undermining women. It is a widespread problem that is seeping into their worlds, so even if they have not witnessed this directly, the chances are they will be experiencing the same message secondhand, within their friend groups or at school.

The issue with blocking this line of conversation at the first instance, is that this is the plot that these men online have already played out to them via their content. "Women, parents and teachers do not want you to know the truth. They will silence you".

So, by shutting your teens down, immediately you are reinstating the narrative by silencing them. "Ahh, he said they would try and do this".

- Let them lead. Instead of showing anger or disgust, even if it feels unnatural, keep calm and pull them into you. Listen. Give them a safe space to be curious, where they will not be judged for their opinion.

- Challenge and probe. Ask why they believe in this opinion, chances are you will likely find some sense and logic in their perspective, so be sure to acknowledge those points and offer a counter perspective. "I see why you would think that however..." "I understand that, have you also considered...".

- Stay connected and calm. If it is a subject you are not well versed in, do some research prior to your conversation if you can. Stay curious.

This level of connection over the big stuff will be much easier if you have practiced debating and listening with your teen over the stuff you needn't sweat. So make it part of a regular go to, to discuss what's going on. What makes them tick? What causes have captured their hearts?

You cannot afford to leave these conversations, comments or actions unchecked, as this allows the misinformation to grow.

Equally though, we can't protect them from everything. We can't make every decision on their behalf so pick your battles. They are not mini versions of us and as such we cannot make them think exactly the way that we do. They are not just our plasticine, to mould as we see fit.

THOUGHT

> Showing love. You can love your children with every fibre of your being, but you have to show them with actions or else they will not feel it.

The struggle is real (and normal)

Feeling like you don't have it all together is completely normal.
Struggle is normal. It's actually sometimes necessary and important.

Rise to the challenge

"Shifting from childhood to teen, I think I was mainly excited for them. Of course I worried a bit, but just kept watching and listening. I enjoyed seeing them change into the adult they would become, the new experiences and friendships they were exposed to and watching them become more confident in themselves. Also they challenged us, as parents and people, to be better."

AROUND THE TABLE

Well it certainly keeps you on your toes this parenting lark doesn't it.

To date, I don't think I have had to keep relearning on the job, at any other stage of parenting or maybe even life, more than I have had to during the shift from child to teen.

I feel like I need new skills every day. I can see my teens changing before my eyes both physically and emotionally.

My phone often generates a photo of the day that I glance at thinking, 'Oh they look so young' or 'Wow they look different there', before I realise it was taken within the past year. It's more than the time flying by, it's puberty of course, as they charge towards adulthood.

Sometimes I wish I had taken a photo a day, just to keep hold of some of those moments, to preserve snapshots in time because as quickly as I get used to this new version of my teen, another is in their place. It's rapid.

More than their faces and bodies changing though, the thing I find hardest is that some days I don't recognise the person they are at all. They have needs that change like the wind, they pull you in and push you away.

They can be arrogant, withdrawn, make bad choices and leave me going to bed at night, questioning everything I have done to date. They make decisions that I never thought they would and they sometimes 'let me down'.

Straight talking now, sometimes teenagers are a massive pain in the arse. But weren't we all during our teenage years?

I am not excusing cruel behaviour or suggesting that we should write off every bad choice throughout teenage years and allocate it to exploration, but I do think my expectations needed to adjust. Maybe I have to reestablish what I am measuring against before I have the right to 'feel let down'. It's no good continuing to treat them like a 10-year old, and expecting them to still be your little cuddly bear is it? They are heading towards being a grown-ass bear now, it makes sense that they have different needs. Even if not so secretly, you still just want nothing more than to snuggle all day.

I also need to pay attention to the incredible parts of having a teenager, of which there are many. Crucially that annoying negative bias affects us all, especially when we are tired, trying to juggle everything or just feeling like it's all a bit much. It's easy to focus on the difficult bits when you are overwhelmed or just fed up with picking up someone else's pants from the bathroom floor for the millionth time.

I have found it hard though, regulating my own feelings. The main thing has been just thinking I have it all figured out, parenting was pretty smooth overall until the teens. It came naturally. Some days now, I feel like I am going backwards. Like I am getting worse at it. Sometimes I feel I am losing my grip completely. I can't be the only one?

As a newborn our daughter was possibly the loudest crier you have ever heard.

In fact, you may have heard her if you lived anything within a 100 mile radius of our home.

We would meticulously tick off potential reasons for the current outburst, you know the drill. Is she tired? Is she hungry? Does she need her nappy changing? Does she have wind? The list went on.

> **What don't your parents understand about you?**
> ❝ Dunno man. They are really annoying.

After a few weeks, we had it pretty nailed, if I do say so myself. A little personalised routine saw our daughter start to sleep through. Until she didn't. She just didn't. No matter how much we followed the routine, no matter how many 'tasks' we ticked off our list. She just wouldn't play ball any more.

I remember my husband turning to me during that phase, slightly panic stricken "I can deal with all the newborn stuff, the nappies, the crying, even the lack of sleep. What I find really tough is the regression. You just think you are getting somewhere and out of nowhere it all changes and you are seemingly right back to the start again."

Back then it didn't bother me. I just accepted that that's the deal with newborns and got on with it. I was happy to just be in for the ride. Finding our way together.

When we first moved into teen years, I just carried on parenting in the same way I had for so many years before, and I expected to get the same results but, in my experience it doesn't work that way. I experienced the same challenges, akin to my daughter's regression. Techniques and experience didn't work with these new versions of my children. I had to start fresh and learn fast.

So yes, as you embark on the teen years there is a shift into a new era, but that is actually really exciting. I love to gamify life, so I try to look at it as levelling up or getting a promotion. Is it optimistic to be planning retirement in the next stage?

The point is, it's an opportunity for reflection for sure, but there is no point in dwelling on what has been. It's time for a new challenge.

It's an opportunity to watch your child, the same one you have nurtured to this point, start to transform into the young adult they will become.

It is not your job now, to mould them into the version of an adult that you want them to be, rather it's time to take a step back and simply be there if they fall. And they will.

They are no longer those little toddlers we scooped up and held after they scraped their knee. I know that however much I want to, I shouldn't rush to pick them up. They need to be able to do that for themselves. That's not to say it isn't hard to resist doing so, especially when you know you have the answers and they don't.

And that's just it, they don't have all the answers yet. They are not 'letting me down' by acting in a way I have not foreseen for them. They are not a picture perfect human nor would I want them to be, no one is.

Between us though, letting go of control is not easy for me. I love my children, more than anything and I will always want to keep them safe. Still, they have to be allowed to make mistakes, they have to be allowed to grow without leading the way now, I will be right behind them instead. Cheering them on (or watching through my fingers).

What I do have control over:

I can be present.
I can show love.
I can choose not to judge them.
I can always have their back.
I can keep turning up.
I can encourage them to step into their truth.
I can remind them to be kind.
I can show kindness to myself.
I can teach them how to regulate emotions.
I can help them to navigate their feelings.
I can encourage confidence.
I can teach them to celebrate and learn from failure.
I can be honest with them.
I can encourage them to be a person they are proud to be.

Until they don't

I wasn't exaggerating my daughter's regression. From 8 months to around 3 years, our daughter decided to wake up almost every night, just for a few moments to check we were there, calling out to us from her bedroom. As she grew older, I would whisper, "Why are you awake?" She would reply "I just need choo".

They seem like they are worlds apart, the little ones I once had and the people I know now.

Teen years don't signal a loss, it's a time of growth and that is exciting.

Instead of mourning the loss of their childhood I have been leaning into what I love about them being older.

Primarily I learn a lot from these humans. New music, new trends, new ways to parent, whilst I can indulge in a nostalgia fest from time to time too. I love introducing them to TV shows I've not rewatched for years, *Gavin and Stacey* has just reentered our realm.

We push each other out of our comfort zones, they can be great company and they challenge me to be a better person.

They give me insights, make me laugh and encourage me to try new things. Of course I sometimes miss them telling me they need me in the middle of the night, but I suspect those calls are just around the corner. It's going to be far less cute when it's under the influence of alcohol at 4 in the morning isn't it.

Remember when

If you want an idea for a 'date night' with your teens, revisiting some highlights from your own youth is a great shout. Roll out the VHS player, dig out your old CDs or make a school disco playlist from your era. Open up conversations about your childhood and theirs. Nostalgia can be connective and nurturing for all involved.

Note of caution; Prepare to be roasted when your favourite childhood film ends up not being quite as amazing as you remember it. I am speaking from experience guys, Indiana Jones and the Temple of Doom is apparently not the spectacular I once thought it was.

At 13 " It's your life to make happen.

The power of (young) love

I remember sitting in front of the fire at my dad's house, pouring my heart into a diary.

I remember writing my initials alongside those of my crush in gel pen on my hand (you did that too right?).

I remember thinking of my boyfriend whenever I listened to a love song on the radio.

And it was real. It felt intense, all consuming, wonderful when all was good, and heartbreaking when it went wrong, four days later.

Young love, it's powerful stuff. Yes it may burn bright for only a moment, but it is a moment that often stays with us forever.

I try hard to not forget that feeling as it stops me from being dismissive of the feelings my teen is experiencing, it stops me short of telling them, it's just a phase.

I try to remember how love felt as a teen myself, and how beautiful it can be, allowing love and infatuation to be your main thought of the day. Do you remember that? Actually, just think of that for a moment. Imagine not having all of the responsibilities that you do now. Imagine just having the time to dream up scenarios and first kisses.

For teens though, that level of passion doesn't just apply to love. In my experience, young people connect and feel deeply. Now we can choose to write it off as too sensitive, over the top, obsessive or single-minded if you prefer, but I like to see it as a strength. One I actually find quite contagious.

My son, when he was small, loved cars. By two, he could name every make of car on the road by its badge, he would spend hours lining up Hot Wheels in various arrangements and earnestly explaining to me that you could tell an Audi because it had rings, and a Peugeot, well that always 'has a lion on it'.

As he grew, cars faded, replaced with the high-octane world of Marvel. There wasn't a superhero in town he couldn't give me the lowdown on. Again, there came a day when these toys and books were packed away, don't get me started, it's giving me *Toy Story* vibes just thinking of it.

Now it's music that has his heart and he feels it deeply. You can forget trying to have a conversation with him whilst there's a beat in the background.

Now I appreciate that this is a personal anecdote, but I am sure that your teens will also have something they connect with. If, in the eyes of the system, it holds academic weight, then that may make things a little easier. Often though, the things we are passionate about are considered by society as curveball or alternative. As parents that can be challenging.

What you choose to support, encourage or ignore is entirely a personal choice.

In our case, it turns out that music isn't much favoured within the mainstream curriculum, here in the UK. It is given far less focus on the timetable compared to other lessons, such as Spanish or Geography. In 2023, only 5,000 students in England took A-level in music, which is a 45% decline from 2010. To compound the lack of support, I recently had a conversation with one of his teachers, who advised me that she believes music is only accessible via nepotism or fluke.

So, I figure I have a couple of options:

A Support my son to go in the direction he wishes, emotionally and financially knowing that music could very well end up, one day, packed up in the same box as the Hot Wheels and superhero figures have been.

B Tell him his dreams should be more realistic.

And then I catch sight of lyrics by The Beatles sketched on the back of his hand, and I remember the gel pens.

> **At 13** " Failure is a part of learning. Never fear it.

They will believe you.

Whether you tell them they are smart.
Or you tell them they are not.

They will believe you.

When you tell them they are able.
Or you tell them they are not.

They will believe you.

The opportunity

I don't know about you but I am starting to find it hard to remember all the details. When I look back through my parenting journey, so much of it fades away or merges together. One memory seeps into another, "Oh yeah, I remember. Was that when we went to the beach? Oh no actually, it was the day we went into that town... I think". The ages of my children when they hit their milestones seems to have plopped straight out of my head, but they were so important at the time.

Lucky for me, I have referenced them with each date noted in their 'babies first' books, for the all important time that I need to know the exact date that my baby ate curry for the first time. Although if we are being honest we know that child number one's book is more dutifully filled out than that of child number two. Because. Time. Sorry second child, I love you just the same.

It would be fair to say I find myself reflecting a lot these days but following my bout of 'grief' as they left their childhoods I started to realise that this time could be pretty rewarding. Not just as a parent but also as me. Just me.

The past 14 years or so have been a whirlwind. A non-stopping production line of parental tasks, career juggling and quite frankly, putting myself last.

As our teens become more self-sufficient in theory there should start to be a little more time to do what we want. Yes I am looking at you.

Ok, so admittedly it hasn't quite panned out like that this week with an additional shop needed due to a growth spurt induced snack-ident, a doctor's appointment, a contraband meeting at the school, a forgotten coat and the observation of holes cut into their sports uniform (so that it can be worn over thumbs, duh).

Both emotionally and physically extra time is just around the corner I am sure of it, but what to do with it? Do I even know who I am when I am not a parent 24/7?

Could it be that that loss of purpose is actually what triggers those feelings of guilt and regret? Is it the thought of having a lack of purpose that heightens the need to hold on to our teens, that makes us wish they were little again?

> ** The only constant in life is change **
> **- Heraclitus**

Time moves on, there is no holding on to it or elongating moments in order to enjoy them for longer. Your teens are growing up. Fact. Will they still be asking for snacks every 10 minutes, probably. Will you end up with a bit more spare time overall, most likely.

So this is your sign to find something for you. Just for you. Having a purpose is a fundamental human need. If, aside from parenting, yours is not obvious then take some time to consider it. Take this time to assess yourself for a moment.

What are you good at? What gives you pleasure? What do you care about?

It could be something artistic, an exercise goal or that you are simply craving some space. You may want to focus on your career, a passion project or your garden. It may be that your marriage needs some additional time, or that you are ready to get back in the dating game. Whatever it is, it is yours to work for.

In fact write it here, with intention. What do you need?

_____

_____

_____

_____

_____

_____

_____

_____

_____

_____

_____

If it is not clear, try some new things. Allow yourself time to sit with yourself to bring focus to your needs. It may take some practice, as you have likely not been the priority for a while.

Dear teen,

I found sleepless nights hard. Yet I miss that newborn bubble and sleepy days with you.

I found being one step ahead a toddler hard. Yet I miss the wonder of discovering something new with you.

I found primary school organisation hard. Yet I miss how excited you were to show me what you had achieved.

I found the constant need to be present hard. Yet I miss you asking to share moments with me as often.

I'm finding the emotional demands of parenting a teen hard. Yet I am forever grateful to be able to be here for you, right now.

At 13

" You have no idea how talented, beautiful and incredible you are. I just need to let her know that she's going to make it basically. I need her to know that she's going to make it and that she is going to make a difference to so many people's lives one day. That all the things that she is afraid of will never happen. They just will never happen. I want her to know that I'm going to be there for her always.

I blame the parents

You have to be understanding, but not a push-over
Available, but not there all the time
To guide them, but not take over
To be there, but not to fix everything
But, if there's something big that needs fixing, you should definitely make sure you're there for that
You need to keep showing up even though most of the time they won't want you there
You need to keep trying, keep learning, keep moving in a world that moves faster than you can keep up with it
You need to let them in to how you're feeling and what is going on in the world to keep them educated and aware, without letting any of this weigh heavy on their shoulders
You need to do enough
But enough seems like a lot, a lot of the time.

What don't your parents understand about you?
❝ When you say sarcastic humour and they don't get it.

It's not your problem

I have brought up our teens, to be independent, resilient and confident. They have been taught from a young age they can be anything they want to be.

And then, they reached their teens and started to be quite literally 'anything they wanted to be', and I discovered this does not always align with everything I (or their schools for that matter) want them to be.
I find myself spending time and energy getting them to 'toe the line'. Restricting them. Should I be? It feels kind of counterintuitive.

I don't have the answer, but I am not sure that 'trouble' is always what society would have us believe it to be.

School is where it hits hardest. It is restrictive in many ways, especially if your teens favour creative endeavours over academic ones or have other challenges, meaning the classroom setting is a hard place for them to be. Homework is a common bone of contention across families I have found.

Quite early on in my parenting journey I was talking with a parent to older children, discussing his take on homework. He described it as a contract between his son, and the school. One that he did not have personal responsibility for.

He could indeed remind his son that he had homework, and summarise what the consequences with the school would be, should his son not complete the tasks set, but it seemed he had made an active choice not to punish his son for not doing his homework. Any consequences were down to the school.

It clicked with me straight away, homework has been a struggle for us and it was causing disagreements and interrupting our quality time on a regular basis.

We, as parents, adopted this mantra from that point on. It seems to have served us well for the most part, meaning we do not have one more thing to think about, and our then young children learnt early on how to manage their own workload.

Don't get me wrong there have been a fair few missed assignments and subsequent detentions along the way, but it is their problem to deal with not mine. Nowadays it is rare that they don't complete it and they know I am here to help if they need it.

I would much prefer to be teaching them how to manage deadlines and responsibility at this stage of their lives when the consequences are ultimately minimal, over spoon-feeding them and then having them learn, quite literally on the job when they leave home.

It is, without a doubt, something that will divide opinion. What do you think? Terrible idea or food for thought?

It is ok to split the room

They are your teens. This is your family. Not everyone will, or needs to like the decisions you make.

If we are all following exactly the same paths and the same set of boundaries, we can expect to all end up pretty much in the same place. That's not what being human is all about, despite what those Silicon Valley executives would have us believe.

The beauty of life, and bringing up a family is in the nuance. It sits in the light and shade that makes us different. Our social feeds have us stuck being fed content that buffers our opinions and often doesn't challenge our thinking. If that is your main source of information and news, consider that you are only seeing one side of the coin.

As a family we travel a fair amount. We have done since the children were young, much to the judgement of many. I have heard it all, from "Aren't you being a bit irresponsible" all the way through to "I don't know why you waste your money on travel, when they won't remember it anyway". The school the children attended were very strict with regards to holiday authorisations and our local council have fined us due to taking our children on holiday in term time. Regardless of society telling us it was a bad idea, we still packed up and left. It is fair to say, not every trip has gone to plan. I had some very serious thinking to do following a trip to Mexico that saw us caught up in a shooting.

It was a few years ago now, and our children had been checked into the children's club for a while, enjoying a Halloween trick or treating experience around the resort. Myself and my husband, having enjoyed some R&R around the pool, headed back to the room to get changed, prior to collecting them.

We were just about to leave the room, when I heard raised voices from outside. To begin with I thought it was a group of young Americans, who had been playing raucously (alright there grandma) in the pool as we left, but the shouting continued to grow. Something was off. I ventured out to our balcony to see what the fuss was about, to see guests running from the beachfront in panic. Something was very, very wrong. Then I heard the words, "There's a shooter".

Terrified for the safety of my children, I called the reception to ensure all the children were back in the clubhouse. They had no idea if they were safe, or not. They actually had no idea where they were.

As crazy as it may seem, my parenting instincts cut in and myself and my husband left our room. Tentatively we crossed the resort, in order to get to our children, who we found were thankfully, safe within the kids club. We spent the next two hours in a safe room, waiting for the all clear from management.

The shooting, it transpired later, was a gang related incident. We, as tourists, were not direct targets, but it was still a terrifying incident to be wrapped up in.

The summary is, despite finding ourselves in a worse case scenario, I don't regret that trip.

Family travel has not always gone to plan. From shootings, to projectile vomiting, the flu and even a monkey bite, I don't regret one single trip. Travelling has been right for our family. Our children have had the opportunity to learn about the world from seeing it with their own eyes, to meet new people and to have a deeper understanding of other cultures and beliefs.

You could be a backpacking single parent, homeschooling around the world or dead set on never stepping out of your own village. You could be career focused, a stay at home parent or juggling a combination of the two. You may travel with your teens or leave them at home whilst you catch the rays. Whatever it is, there will be others who do the opposite. There will always be someone to tell you you are doing it wrong. Just stay in your lane. Do you. Do what's best for your family. Try not to spread judgement to others that are not doing it your way. Get busy living your own life.

> ## At 13
> " You don't have to be an adult yet.

There is no gain in spreading shame

Keep your teen's private issues private. If they have trusted you enough to talk with you about a mistake, issue or even a love interest, don't bring it up around others or worse, post it on social media. Certainly don't mock them or laugh at their decisions. Otherwise, why would they choose to trust you again?

> We had a very difficult few years and if I could turn back the clock I would want to find a way for us to talk more openly to one another. I wish I had given him the opportunity to speak to me about anything.
>
> **AROUND THE TABLE**

Developing the CV of life

My husband and I have run a marketing agency for nearly 20 years, employing several people, so between us we are pretty familiar with the recruitment process.

Over the past 15 years or so, we have found ourselves paying less and less attention to CVs and the previous work experience of candidates, building our team instead, based on strength of character and emotional intelligence, over professional skill sets.

I suspect as technology continues to become more prominent in our workspaces, with AI and automation starting to dominate many industries, personality led hiring will become the norm. After all, if you only need a handful of actual humans, you best ensure they are filling the gaps that technology cannot.

Beyond the corporate world, these skills are also a vital building block in becoming an adult who is able to make their own choices, be able to prioritise their wellbeing and have their own opinions, whilst showing compassion and kindness to others. As such I have been trying to build up my teen's 'CV of life' by diversifying and honing their interpersonal skills in ways that you would not necessarily be able to learn in school.

Skills such as empathy, black box thinking, decision making, debating, honesty, enough confidence to get their voice heard, knowing the right questions to ask, listening and how to foster a positive mindset.

Find ways to encourage the skill sets that you value, in a fun and accessible way.

For example, if you want to encourage public speaking then look for activities or clubs that assist with that. The obvious go-to would be to attend a drama club or something similar, but there is also plenty of opportunity much closer to home. Play games that cause individuals to have to speak up or act, such as two truths, one lie, or charades. Set up a family karaoke night. Even holding family meetings and allowing each person a chance to speak and be listened to, will start to build strength within that skill.

We tick many of these boxes by expanding our comfort zones.

Dear teen,

Picture you are standing in the dark. You reach out your hands and spin in a circle, the area that you have touched lights up as if covered by a powerful spotlight or warmed by the sun. That area is your comfort zone.

We wander from time to time into the darkness when we try something new and venture into the unknown, and it can feel scary of course, but the light arrives pretty much as soon as we do. And that in itself is pretty special.

Just like reaching a new level on a game, and watching your map expand, the next time we head in that direction it doesn't seem nearly as daunting because the light is already on and we are familiar with the journey.

Yes, the moment just before the light comes on can be scary, but it can also be thrilling. Find joy in it.

Much of life is all about expanding those comfort zones and dipping into the unknown. The more light we invite in, the stronger we become.

You are not small

It is all too easy as a parent to belittle our own role or needs.

I realised a few years back that I was often making my needs the smallest in the room, but I have been making a conscious effort to adjust that.

I want to raise both of my teens to be able to hold their own power, to have a voice and yet, in order to make life comfortable for them, I often make my own voice smaller. It strikes me that minimising my needs is not the right example to set.

I will give you an example, I recently had to go away for work, just a flyby into London and I intended on staying a couple of nights in order to get some writing done too, away from distractions and regular life.

My daughter asked me why I was staying and I explained the importance of the trip and why I needed to focus on my writing, that there was a deadline and the quality of my work was important to me. She got it.

In the past, I would have found myself saying "Sadly I have to attend a meeting" or "I am sorry I have to go, it's annoying but I will be back as soon as I can". I have been trying to reframe it for a few reasons. One, if you are leaving your family, even if only for a short while, is it not better for them to understand it is for something worthwhile, rather than something you put little value on? Otherwise, why would you be choosing it over precious time with them?

Secondly, if I want my teens to have their own purpose and attach a value to it in the future, then it is good to model that I too have elements of my life that hold weight. Something that is mine alone.

It doesn't need to be a career or a project, it could be an exercise class, finishing a book or spending time with your friends. It is a form of self-care, but it is also setting a good example.

Fast forward to your teen in their 20s and I think you would be disappointed if they were continually putting their own needs at the bottom of the pile.

What don't your parents understand about you?

❝ They don't understand what I feel and they don't listen without shouting.

Choices

I love listening to the opinions of teens. Genuinely.

I find it fascinating to listen to their point of view. That's their POV for all you young ones reading this. It is really easy as a parent to just make all the decisions, however (and you can read this bit quietly if you prefer) you don't always have the best ideas.

I have started to look for ways to include our teens in the decision making a bit more around the house and in day to day life. I figure it is not going to be that long until they are roaming freely in the world, so best get some practice in.

We have been fortunate to be able to travel as a family ever since we became one, and as a former travel agent (a long, long time ago) I tend to be the one that picks and organises where we go.

This year I decided to approach it differently. I set everyone up with a challenge. I gave a budget and a time of year we would be travelling to each member of our family. Then I set them the task of researching a great destination. It was the perfect opportunity to practice some skills they have learnt over the years in a real life format. Although I would be lying if I said I wasn't a bit nervous about where we could end up.

We all set to budgeting, destination research, consideration for suitability for all travellers, then each had to create a presentation to gain votes for our chosen holiday of choice.

If I am being honest, I thought my pick was a shoo-in and then came the pitching.

True to form, our teens are very different, so naturally, so too were their pitches. One opted for a fully designed presentation, beautifully displayed on the TV, accompanied by a distinguished and persuasive sales chatter, complete with FAQs and time at the end for additional questions.

The other created an equally engaging masterpiece, by making up a rap covering all the finer points of their chosen destination.

Safe to say, I didn't win the vote.

> **At 13** " You can learn anything, and be whoever you want to be.

Q: What would your teen-self not forgive you for, if you hadn't done it in your lifetime.

Secondly... have you done it yet?

Enjoy the ride

Let's all ignite the FUN and bring the silly. Stop taking everything so damn seriously.

Think of a funny, weird or energising challenge you can set for the week ahead.

Dance, sing and actively bring light into the house. It will soon be reflected back at you.

What don't your parents understand about you?
❯❯ They think I am addicted to my phone, but I'm not.

Walking through the woods

You made the wrong call?
Own it.

Another parent went out of their way to tell me something about my teen last week. It was something they thought I didn't know, but I did. Therefore, thankfully despite their smugness I wasn't blindsided. Nor did I think the revelation was a huge deal. Some poor judgement on my teens part sure, but no harm was done to anyone or anything, just a mistake. One that we had already discussed as a family. I wasn't about to reopen the case, Your Honour. I did feel pretty judged though. I felt them watching me, waiting for a bigger reaction. A little bit of anticipation in the air, you know. Waiting for me to fill the gap. To tell them what the course of punishment was due to be for my wretched teenager.

Actually, even initially it wasn't something that felt like a big issue and I certainly didn't feel the need to discuss it further with said judgey parent. Come to think of it, I don't really know why I am including this little anecdote, maybe just for solidarity's sake. Maybe because it is still a little raw. Maybe just to acknowledge that you needn't explain your parenting choices to others. To note that however hard you try, you can't always keep total control of your teens behaviour or their choices.

For me it is easy to visualise walking through the woods. There may be a path that you always take, a familiar route.

That may be the path your teen decides to take too.

Sometimes though they will wander from the path. You will find out about choices they have made, decisions that you don't agree with and things that leave you sad or disappointed. That doesn't serve either of you. Your teen has to wander in the figurative undergrowth sometimes, to work out where they need to end up, and the chances are it won't be on the path you have marked out for them.

So relax. Just keep on enjoying your own path, and watch on from there. Make sure they know where you are should they need to come back, give them directions before they leave, even hand them a torch if you like, but trust they will find their own path in good time.

At 13 " Be kind.

Getting it right

A repeated mistake I make as a parent is considering my teens 'grown'. They are so far from the little dots they once were, that I fall into the trap of thinking they are good to go. They are funny, smart and engaging in conversations. I make the assumption that they can reason, foresee and fully understand the implications of their actions.

Truth is, I don't often get decision making spot on myself. Do you? So isn't it curious that I so often find myself thinking that they should have got it right the first time.

What was the biggest challenge you faced as a teen?

It's all about confidence

One of the most rewarding parts of bringing up teenagers is seeing them step into their power as they find their way. Building confidence isn't something that happens overnight, it is stitched together day after day by positive language, behaviour and encouragement.

Celebrate the journey, not just the result. Acknowledge the hard work it has taken to get to where they are, whether it is practicing for an audition and not getting the part or making the team, only to end up losing the match.

Instead of simply showering them with praise all the time, first ask your teen how they feel about their achievements, and then offer your own congratulations. This allows them to grow in their own self-confidence and vindication, rather than creating a pattern whereby they only perform to gain the praise of others.

Encourage teens to step out of their comfort zone by diversifying their skills. Try a new club or practice a new skill, rather than just focusing on their main strengths.

Practice what you preach. It is ok to show that you are scared to try something new, providing you go ahead and do it anyway.

Hey you, chatty Cathy. Stop speaking for them in social situations. Zip it in restaurants or during introductions to new people and let your teens take the lead. Celebrate success as a family, even the small wins deserve a big whoop.

Here for it, mess and all

What have you done this week that has caused you to judge yourself harshly? If we tuned in to just a fraction of the voices around us, I am sure we would all find reason to believe we are 'spoiling, poisoning or generally ruining our children'.

It's nonsense.

Most of us are just going through parenting doing the best we can. The world is changing in many ways, often faster than we can keep up with it.

I will give you a real world example. We got our very first dog, Arlo, around 7 years ago. Our friends have just got their first puppy, Paddington. We visited the lovely little ball of fluff during his first week in his new home and I observed something interesting.

Despite all the research, the social media input and the very best intentions, at least 25% of the things we did for Arlo as a puppy are now redundant.

"Get a cage" they said. Now a cage is mean, you should get a pen.

"Feed him kibble not wet food", they said. Now it is down with the wet food, up with the raw.

And yet, our dog is great.

He is a happy, lovable and healthy addition to our family unit.

And yes, I see how it could be seen as hypocritical, from the author of a 'parenting book' to be telling other parenting experts to pipe down, but that's the whole point.

It is not a guide. It is not a set of rules. It's just thoughts, ideas and information, for you to take or leave as you see fit. If you diligently followed everything I have discussed throughout our time together, I can't imagine that would work out.

Parenting is an ever changing landscape. It is probably the most exclusively personal experience you will ever have. You are bringing up and living with another human being, who has their own personality, thoughts and feelings. As they grow, you cannot control how they will respond or act, you cannot control what they will become or what will bring them joy or sorrow. You can't even control if they will like you. You know that.

Granted, you have some control over the environment in which you bring them up, your boundaries and techniques you use, but you dont really know what will work and what won't. That primarily is what this journey together within these pages has been about. Consideration, curiosity and shifting out any judgement.

I am quite sure that to some, this book will have been a messy, contradiction of parenting techniques. But life is a messy affair and parenting is one of the messiest parts of all, because there is no rehearsal.

ff I am still learning 🥮
- Michelangelo

If reading this book has supported you, inspired you or made you question the way in which you are parenting day to day, then I have achieved what I set out to do. Writing it has certainly made me think about the way I am parenting. It is just good to take stock sometimes, isn't it.

It has been a cathartic and exploratory process. It has kept me curious during a time when I was not sure I could do it. Caught in a moment, I wasn't sure if I had, so far, been successful at being a parent, or that I would be able to do a good enough job going forward. I would have really liked to hear someone else admit that. So that is what I am doing for you.

I am not an expert nor a perfect person. I am just a parent.

I love my children and yet I am not always sure I am getting it right.

I am not even sure I know what 'right' is most of the time, but I am choosing curiosity over fear.

I implore you to keep doing the same.

Acknowledgements

No book is a creation of one person alone, so there are a fair few thank you's to be made.

Firstly to the two people that made the entire concept of this book possible, F&E. Thank you for keeping me on my toes, asking ALL the questions and continually challenging me to stay curious. I am so proud of you both.

To Ian, who always lifts me up. Thank you for your love, encouragement and pragmatism in pursuit of my idealism, which has given me everything I needed to get this book written. I love working out life alongside you. Oh, and of course thank you for secretly booking the trip that led to this next part of our adventure.

To Suzi, thank you for your faith in me. Whether it is fate, chance or something else that brought us together, I do not know, but I am very grateful to have met you.

To the entire Synergy family but particularly Cam and Amy, thank you for welcoming me in, I am very excited to see where the journey takes us.

To the friends, family and strangers who have spoken to me throughout the writing process, thank you for your time and honesty.

To my mum, who will likely be the only one who wants a signed copy and an apology to my dad, whose calls have been ignored many times, when I have been 'in the zone'.

To the Gurneys and Ian (again), who have listened to me on countless New Year's Eves, stating that "this year will be the year I publish a book". Thank you for your patience and continued encouragement. I will shut up now. Maybe.